T0286825

CRICKET'S
50
MOST IMPORTANT MOMENTS

CRICKET'S 50

MOST IMPORTANT MOMENTS

TIM EVERSHED

First published by Pitch Publishing, 2023

Pitch Publishing
9 Donnington Park,
85 Birdham Road,
Chichester,
West Sussex,
PO20 7AJ
www.pitchpublishing.co.uk
info@pitchpublishing.co.uk

A CIP catalogue record is available for this book
from the British Library.

ISBN 978 1 80150 504 8

Typesetting and origination by Pitch Publishing
Printed and bound in India by Thomson Press

Contents

Acknowledgements

THE STORY of cricket has been recorded over the centuries by many dedicated historians, journalists and statisticians. I was fortunate that during the writing of this book I was able to call upon their works. There are too many to list here, but they all have my sincere gratitude.

My thanks also go to Steve LeMottee and all the volunteers at Trent Bridge's Peter Wynne-Thomas Library. I was incredibly fortunate to be able to call upon this wonderful treasure trove of cricket books for my research.

Finally, thanks to my wife Hayley for her love, support, help and patience throughout this project.

Introduction

CRICKET HAS come a long way since its beginnings as a pastime for boys in sleepy English villages centuries ago. It is now a global game, played and watched by millions of people around the world. This book charts cricket's journey through the centuries using 50 key moments in the sport's rich history.

Cricket's 50 Most Important Moments begins almost 300 years ago with the codification of the game's laws, which would go through key revisions in the following decades as batting and bowling techniques evolved.

This book looks at the spread of the game across England and beyond as the British Empire helped to export it around the world. We will examine the brief. but crucial role played by North America in the sport's development before more familiar participants including Australia, South Africa and India made their mark on the game.

As the sun set on the British Empire, teams including New Zealand, the West Indies, Pakistan, Sri Lanka and others joined to take those playing Tests to the current number. Each of these has added something unique to the sport through new techniques, star players and different playing conditions.

This book looks at how the sport has developed from the beginnings of first-class matches and the birth of Test cricket, to World Cups and the phenomenon of Twenty20 cricket.

It includes moments from the cricketing geniuses who astonished crowds with their prowess and redefined what was possible. The book also documents some of the incredible matches, series, tours and tournaments that have left lasting legacies on the sport and propelled players to new levels of fame

Cricket's 50 Most Important Moments chronicles the sport's long, colourful and sometimes controversial history by delving into the most significant moments that have happened on and off the cricket field. It also assesses the tactical changes, technological developments and other innovations that have shaped cricket from its infancy to the modern era.

This book presents the 50 moments chronologically rather than attempting to rank them by order of importance. The list is not intended to be definitive and readers will have their own lists. Instead, *Cricket's 50 Most Important Moments* tries to document cricket's growth through these moments and help us understand how the sport became what it is today.

1

The Laws of Cricket *(1744)*

MOST CRICKET fans know that the sport is governed by laws rather than rules. Today, there are 42 Laws of Cricket, which have evolved over time to help create the modern game.

Games resembling the modern sport of cricket have been played in England for centuries. What began as a pastime for boys was increasingly played by adults too.

However, the games themselves, and the laws that governed them, varied from area to area. However, as cricket attracted more and more gamblers, who were playing for higher and higher stakes, the need to establish a universally accepted codification of the laws increased.

In 1744 the Laws of Cricket were agreed for the first time. Although they have been subject to many revisions since, including major changes, such as leg before wicket (lbw) and overarm bowling, many of the 1744 laws remain largely unchanged in the modern game. As such the agreeing of the first Laws of Cricket remains a watershed moment in the development of the sport.

Prior to these laws, rules were generally agreed by the participants in advance of a given match. Eventually, verbal agreements began to give way to written Articles of Agreement.

These provided agreement on likely areas of dispute, an important consideration when significant sums of money were often at stake. Gambling was rife amongst the English aristocracy in the 18th century. They assembled their own teams and challenged their contemporaries to matches for large sums of money.

The handwritten Articles of Agreement from two matches organised by the Duke of Richmond and Viscount Midleton in the summer of 1727 are kept in the West Sussex Record Office. This is the first time that rules are known to have been formally agreed.

The articles are a list of 16 points that are largely recognisable today although not identical to the modern game. Batsmen will be out if the ball is caught, including behind the wicket.

However, the match was played by 12 on each team on a pitch that was 23 yards long and the batsmen had to touch the 'Umpire's Stick' in order to complete a run.

Then, in 1744, a meeting, between the 'noblemen and gentlemen members of the London Cricket Club' – which was based at the Artillery Ground – and other players from various cricket clubs, at the Star and Garter public house in Pall Mall agreed the first Laws of Cricket. The earliest known code of laws was enacted in 1744 but not actually printed, so far as it is known, until 1755.

Today they are preserved on the edge of a handkerchief, which is housed in the Melbourne Cricket Club's museum, entitled *The Laws of the Game of Cricket*. In small text, the laws surround a scene of an early cricket match. The central illustration, a reproduction of Francis Hayman's painting *Cricket in Mary-le-bone Fields*, is considered one of the earliest known depictions of cricket. In it the batsmen wield curved bats in front of wickets with just two stumps, the bowler is poised to release an underhand delivery and two umpires stand on the field.

Like the 1727 Articles of Agreement, these laws are also a mixture of points that remain true today and those that will feel alien to the modern cricketer. The pitch has now been reduced to the 22 yards that remains in use today while the two stumps must be 22 inches high with a six-inch bail. According to the specifications laid out, the ball must weigh between five and six ounces while overs lasted only four balls.

A bowling crease is to be marked in line with the wicket with a popping crease three feet and ten inches in front of it. If the bowler's back foot goes in front of the bowling crease a no-ball is the penalty for overstepping.

The umpire is allowed a certain amount of discretion and it is made clear that the umpire is the 'sole judge' and that 'his determination shall be absolute'. Umpires cannot give a batsman out if the fielders do not appeal. They must allow two minutes for a new batsman to arrive at the wicket and ten minutes between innings.

Methods of dismissal include hitting the ball twice and obstructing the field while the wicketkeeper is required to be still and quiet until the ball is bowled.

One area not covered by the 1744 Laws was bowling actions. Most bowlers would have rolled or skimmed deliveries along the ground at this time although this omission left the door open for pitched deliveries to develop in the coming years.

While anyone familiar with cricket will recognise the game described through the laws, there are some surprising omissions. There is no explanation of how a game is won or how many times a team may bat. Presumably these would have been agreed between the players beforehand.

The 1744 Laws of Cricket met the need for a consistent framework of regulations as the sport grew in popularity.

Further meetings at, first at the Star and Garter and later the Marylebone Cricket Club, which remains the custodian of the Laws of Cricket to this day, would continue to revise the rules. However, it was the first agreed, unified code that created the template on which the modern sport of cricket could later develop and evolve.

2

Play starts at Hambledon *(1750)*

IN 1750 a small parish team from the village of Hambledon in Hampshire began playing cricket matches. Within just a few years this village team had developed into the most important cricket club in England.

In fact, Hambledon regularly took on and beat All-England XIs during its glory years in the 18th century. Its impressive list of cricketing alumni had a profound impact on the sport of cricket, helping develop the laws, evolve tactics and innovate new skills and techniques.

According to H.S. Altham in *A History of Cricket*, Hambledon was 'universally acknowledged' as 'The Cradle of Cricket'.

Altham wrote: 'To the men of Hambledon glory enough remains: if they did not "find out cricket", they raised the game into an art ... in exalting the club of a remote village until it was more than a match for All-England, they wrote a story that reads like a romance.'

That romantic history and reputation still draws cricket fans from around the world to the historic ground at Broadhalfpenny Down and the Bat & Ball pub where club meetings were once held. It was also the inspiration for the first significant cricket book, *The Cricketers of My Time* by John Nyren, the son of Richard Nyren, who was one of the Hambledon club's first captains and great players.

The story that began in 1750 took further shape six years later when Hambledon took on the long-established Dartford club at the Artillery Ground in a series of three matches. In 1764, the club met Chertsey with 'great sums of money depending' while three years after that it recorded two victories by the 'unprecedented margins' of 262 and 224 notches.

It was during the period between 1770 and 1787 that Hambledon 'reigned supreme', according to Altham. In 1772, a Hampshire XI won by 53 runs against an England XI on Hambledon's pitch at Broadhalfpenny Down, a match which is widely regarded as cricket's inaugural first-class match.

According to John Nyren, Hambledon played against an England XI on 51 occasions and were victorious in 29 of these matches.

A year earlier, Hambledon had been involved in a controversy during a match against Chertsey played at Laleham Burway in Surrey. The game was played for high stakes, originally £50 a side, but with larger stakes accruing when, during the first Chertsey innings, Thomas White 'tried to use a bat that was fully as wide as the wicket itself'.

Although there was nothing in the laws of the game to prevent White from using this bat, the Hambledon players objected. Hambledon went on to win the match by a single run but two days later their players made a formal complaint.

Star bowler Thomas Brett, captain Richard Nyren and batsman John Small, who was also a bat maker, all signed the club minutes requesting that bat sizes be restricted to four and a quarter inches. The law was formally changed three years later and the standard remains four and a quarter inches to this day.

In 1775, Small was involved in another incident that would have lasting repercussions for cricket. Small was batting for Hambledon against Kent at the Artillery Ground and facing Edward 'Lumpy' Stevens, the premier bowler of the day. Three times in the course of his second innings, Small was beaten only for the ball to pass through the two-stump wicket each time without hitting the stumps or the bail. As a result, the middle stump was introduced, although it was some years before its use became universal.

This change led to Small, who scored the earliest known century later in 1775, altering the style of the bats he was making from the curved blades visible in early pictures of cricket matches to a 'straightened and shouldered blade'. It also meant that batsmen evolved their technique to a 'straight and defensive' style.

The foundations of this style were laid by Small, along with other great Hambledon batsmen like Billy Beldham and Tom Walker. Beldham's career spanned the 1782 to 1821 seasons and is one of the longest on record by a top-class player.

Walker, who was known as 'Old Everlasting', was noted for his outstanding defensive play and was notoriously difficult to dismiss. On one occasion he faced 170 deliveries from David Harris and scored one run. He is also credited with pioneering roundarm bowling, the predecessor of modern overarm bowling (see Moment 4).

Meanwhile, Hambledon's Tom Sueter was renowned as one of the finest attacking batsmen of the time. He was one of the first batsmen to move his feet, at a time when many deemed it a heresy to leave the crease, as well as one of the pioneers of the cut shot. Sueter was also a top-class wicketkeeper.

There was talent on the bowling side too, led by Brett who was one of the earliest fast bowlers to play cricket, despite playing in the era of underarm bowling. John Nyren described Brett as 'beyond all comparison, the fastest as well as straitest bowler that ever was known'.

Another Hambledon bowler, known only as Lamborn, is widely recognised as the inventor of the off-break. The natural way for an underarm bowler to spin the ball is the leg-break, spinning the ball from the leg side and towards the off side of a right-handed batsman.

Lamborn spun the ball from off to leg against the right-hander. John Nyren wrote that Lamborn was 'the first I remember who introduced this deceitful and teasing style of delivering the ball'.

According to Altham, Harris was the last and greatest of the Hambledon bowlers. He was a fast, accurate underarm bowler who got 'pace off the pitch' with many batsmen receiving injured hands from balls that trapped their unprotected fingers against the bat handle.

However, Hambledon's great days were numbered. Throughout the 1780s there was a shift towards London which became entrenched when Lord's was established as the home of the new Marylebone Cricket Club in 1787.

Although Hambledon reverted to the role of an English village cricket club in the following years, its heyday was immortalised by the Rev. Reynell Cotton's 'Cricket Song'.

Then fill up your glass! – He's the best that drinks the most;
Here's the Hambledon Club! Who refuses the toast?
Let us join in the phrase of the Bat and Wicket,
And sing in full chorus the Patrons of Cricket.

3

Leg before wicket becomes law *(1774)*

THERE ARE ten methods of dismissal facing a batter in cricket but none causes as much debate or controversy as leg before wicket (lbw).

The lbw law is commonly misinterpreted and over the years has caused many problems between bowlers, batters, umpires and the cricketing authorities. Decisions have sometimes sparked crowd trouble and rioting. However, the introduction of lbw gave an advantage to the skilful bowler and as a consequence forced batters to alter their technique. Since its introduction the number of lbw dismissals has risen steadily through the years.

In 1774, the Laws of Cricket were revised by a committee meeting at the Star and Garter pub in London. As well as a number of aristocratic cricket patrons, the committee included representatives from Kent, Hampshire, Surrey, Sussex and London.

It had been 30 years since the original Laws of Cricket had been codified (see Moment 1) and developments in the game had prompted the need to revise them. These included a maximum width for bats, following the 'Monster' bat incident of 1771, and a stipulation that bowlers had one foot behind the bowling crease at delivery.

The main development was the introduction of lbw as a means of dismissal. This was needed because the practice of stopping the ball with the leg had arisen as a negative response to the pitched delivery.

Lbw sees a batter dismissed if, following an appeal by the fielding side, the umpire rules that the ball would have struck the wicket, but was instead intercepted by any part of the batter's body – except a hand holding the bat.

Ultimately, the umpire's decision will depend on a number of criteria, which is where the misunderstandings and controversy often stem from. These include where the ball pitched, whether the ball hit in line with the wickets, the ball's expected trajectory after hitting the batsman, and whether the batter was playing a shot.

The lbw law had become necessary due to the changes in bats and batting techniques since 1744. When the original laws were written curved bats were used by batters, who would generally stand wide of the wicket using a stance that looked closer to those used in baseball.

As bats became straighter so did methods of play, with batters standing closer to the wickets and playing straight shots. However, many batters became proficient at deliberately obstructing the ball from hitting the wickets by using their legs.

Such tactics were criticised by many and so the 1774 laws ruled that the batter was out if they deliberately stopped the ball from hitting the wicket with their leg. The lbw law has gone through many revisions since its introduction. In 1788, the requirement for umpires to decide whether the batter was intentionally obstructing the ball was removed while in 1823 a condition was added that 'the ball must be delivered in a straight line to the wicket'.

The law was extended in 1935 so that a batter could be dismissed lbw even if the ball pitched outside the line of off stump. In the 1970s it was revised again so batters could be out lbw in some circumstances if they did not attempt to hit the ball with their bat.

More recently, video replays and ball-tracking technology to assist umpires have increased the percentage of lbws in major matches. However, the accuracy of the technology and the consequences of its use remain a matter of much debate and discussion.

Without doubt the introduction of lbw back in 1774 changed the game of cricket. It altered the balance of the contest between bowler and batter, offering rewards for skill from the former and prompting changes in techniques from the latter. It has also fuelled countless hours of debate between cricketing fans.

4

Roundarm bowling is legalised *(1835)*

IN 1835, the Marylebone Cricket Club (MCC) bowed to the inevitable and amended the Laws of Cricket to make roundarm bowling legal. This change spelt the end for the dominance of underarm bowling and set cricket firmly on the path to the overarm techniques that remain prevalent to this day.

The 1835 law said: 'If the hand be above the shoulder in the delivery, the umpire must call "No Ball".'

The arguments over roundarm bowling had raged for much of the previous 40 years with a law specifically prohibiting the style introduced just 19 years earlier in 1816. Although the beginnings of roundarm bowling are subject to debate the technique quickly became predominant and opened up the way to overarm bowling.

The development of the roundarm style saw a number of players experimenting with their bowling techniques, including Tom Walker and John Willes, who were both key in its evolution.

Walker was more famous as a batsman with an exceptional defensive technique. He played for the Hambledon club, as well as Hampshire and Surrey. He also narrowly missed out on being the first man to score two centuries in a first-class match when he scored 95 not out and 102 against Kent in 1786.

Walker was also a decent bowler who claimed at least 337 wickets in 197 recorded matches. Roundarm was developed during Hambledon's winter training sessions in a barn. Walker worked out that he could generate more bounce and variation of pace if he bowled with his arm away from his body. These deliveries added to the problems facing batsmen on the poor pitches of the day.

However, trials in matches ended with Walker being called for no-balls and in the end his own club banned him from the practice.

'About a couple of years after Walker had been with us, he began the system of throwing instead of bowling, now so much the fashion. At that time, it was esteemed foul play, and so it was decided by a council of the Hambledon Club which was called for the purpose,' wrote John Nyren in his book *The Hambledon Men*.

Despite this decision, roundarm persisted and was controversial enough to cause the 1816 change to the Laws of Cricket.

It said: 'The ball must be bowled (not thrown or jerked), and be delivered underhand, with the hand below the elbow. But if the ball be jerked, or the arm extended from the body horizontally, and any part of the hand be uppermost, or the hand horizontally extended when the ball is delivered, the Umpires shall call, "No Ball".'

Regardless, roundarm continued to be used with bowlers claiming it was a reaction to the dominance of batsmen at the time.

One leading proponent was Willes, who is said to have noticed how effective the style was when used by his sister Christiana. According to some versions of the story, when Christiana was bowling to her brother in the garden at home in the 1800s, she found herself inconvenienced by her large, lead-weighted dress which prevented her from performing the underarm action. Lifting her arm to just above waist height allowed her to bowl without interference from her attire.

Willes realised that the pace and bounce generated by this raised-arm action made the delivery potentially more difficult to play than a conventional underarm one, so he adopted the style himself.

On 15 July 1822, in the MCC versus Kent match at Lord's, Willes opened the bowling for Kent and was promptly no-balled for using his roundarm action. He reportedly threw the ball away and left Lord's, not only withdrawing from the match but retiring from cricket altogether.

However, the style of bowling persisted and arguments continued to rage. Five years later Sussex took on an All-England team in a series of roundarm trial matches. Sussex were the best county side in England at the time and owed much of their success to bowlers William Lillywhite and Jem Broadbridge, both of whom would bowl roundarm when allowed to by the presiding umpires.

Sussex won the first match by seven wickets in Sheffield and the second at Lord's by three wickets. The All-England side objected to Sussex's roundarm bowling and threatened to boycott the third match. Eventually they relented and won the final rubber by 27 runs, but only after allowing their own bowlers to use the style.

In 1828, following the Sussex versus All-England roundarm trials, MCC modified Law 10 to permit the bowler's hand to be raised as high as the elbow. However, this measure failed to stop the arguments surrounding the roundarm style and in 1835 the sport's de facto governing body made it legal.

Although some bowlers did persist with underarm following the change to the law, it was roundarm that soon dominated. Leading exponents included W.G. Grace, John Jackson and Alfred Mynn, who had been mentored by Willes.

Following the legalisation of roundarm, bowlers continued to raise the height of their arm when delivering the ball. Many began to raise the hand above the shoulder and were no-balled.

History began to repeat itself, especially when Surrey played an All-England side in 1862. This time it was the All-England team whose bowlers were pushing the boundaries. And, after their bowler Edgar Willsher was no-balled six times, the team's nine professionals staged a walk-off.

Two years later MCC once again rewrote Law 10 to allow the bowler to bring their arm through at any height providing the arm was kept straight and the ball was not thrown. This completed the evolution of bowling and 1864 is often said to mark the beginning of modern cricket. However, it was the 1835 decision that allowed roundarm bowling which laid the groundwork for further changes to the laws and styles of bowling.

5

The first international match *(1844)*

St George's Cricket Club, New York City, 24–26 September 1844
Canada tour of USA

Canada	USA
82	64
Winckworth, Sharpe, Freeling 12	Tinson 14
Wright 5 wickets	Winckworth, French 4 wickets
63	58
Winckworth 14	Turner 14
Groom 5 wickets	Sharpe 6 wickets

Canada won by 23 runs

IT WILL come as a surprise to many cricket fans that the oldest international fixture in the sport was played between the USA and Canada. The fixture was first played in 1844 and continues to this day.

Cricket was amongst the sports spread through its colonies by the British Empire and was being played in Australia, New Zealand, southern Africa and the Indian subcontinent, as well as Canada and the USA.

The first international match was played at St George's Cricket Club in midtown Manhattan, New York City between teams billed as the 'United States of America versus the British Empire's Canadian Province'. The Canadians won the first match between the two North American countries by 23 runs.

The international fixture was played 33 years before England and Australia played the first Test match in Melbourne but had its origins four years earlier than that.

In 1840, St George's had been invited to tour Canada and play Toronto Cricket Club. However, when the 18-strong touring party arrived in Toronto they found their hosts were not expecting them as the invitation had been sent by an imposter.

Regardless of the error, a match was quickly arranged for the tourists, who won by ten wickets. Despite the short notice the match was deemed a success; it had attracted a good attendance including the governor of Upper Canada, and a return match was arranged.

The return would be played in New York and teams were to be selected from players from across each country rather than single club sides. Clubs from Philadelphia, Washington DC and Boston, as well as New York, were represented in the US team. The Canadian team invited players from Toronto, Guelph Cricket Club and Upper Canada College.

The match took place between 24 and 26 September 1844, as bad weather extended it from the scheduled two days into a third day, and attracted 20,000 spectators. It is also estimated $100,000 to $120,000 worth of bets were placed on the match.

The USA bowled out Canada for 82 in 32 overs in their first innings after winning the toss and electing to field. Samuel Wright took five wickets while three Canadian batsmen shared the top score of 12. At the end of the first day the US were 61/9 in reply as Robert Tinson top-scored with 14 while David Winckworth and Fred French took four wickets apiece.

After the second day was washed out the USA added only three runs to their score before losing their final wicket.

Canada were bowled out for 63 in their second innings with Henry Groom taking five wickets for the hosts. Winckworth top-scored with 14 runs as Canada set the USA a victory target of 82 in their second innings. George Sharpe was the pick of the Canadian bowling attack as the USA were all out for 58 to give Canada a 23-run victory.

The match was such a success that a return was arranged in Montreal the following year. Canada once again ran out winners, this time by 61 runs. The fixture between the two countries is now played for the Auty Cup, although it is not played every year. At the time of writing in 2023, it is held by the USA following their 33rd win in 2017.

6

William Clarke's All-England XI
(1846)

THE ALL-ENGLAND XI was a professional, travelling team that comprised the best cricketing talent of the day after being founded by Nottinghamshire's William Clarke in 1846.

The team took advantage of the opportunities offered by the newly developed railways to travel around the country taking on local teams for money. It also tapped into changes in society following the Reform Act and helped to break the stranglehold the Marylebone Cricket Club (MCC) had over professional players.

The All-England XI was also the forerunner of international Test teams and it supplied many of the players for the first English team to tour overseas in 1859. Clarke's vision for this team changed the face of cricket forever.

Clarke was the team's captain, manager, agent, leading bowler, talent-spotter and promoter. He was also an underarm bowler, who used a slow, leg-spin delivery to great effect and resisted the change to the roundarm style that was becoming more popular during his playing career.

From 1847 to 1853, he averaged 340 wickets a season, peaking when he dismissed 476 batsmen in the final one of those seasons. Clarke died in 1856 after playing 41 seasons in first-class cricket and obtaining a wicket with the last ball he bowled. In total, he took 2,382 wickets for the All-England XI.

Clarke was born in Nottingham in 1798, playing his first game for the county in 1816 when only 17 and progressing on to captain the side 14 years later. Clarke was also a publican and after marrying the landlady of the Trent Bridge Inn he used the ground behind to create an enclosed cricket pitch that could be used as Nottinghamshire's new home.

He played in the inaugural North versus South match at Lord's in 1836 and nine years later became one of the ground staff there as an MCC employee. Despite enjoying an excellent season with the ball Clarke was unhappy with the pay on offer to MCC's ground staff.

His response was to found the All-England XI in 1846. The team was made up of the best English professional players of the time, as well as two nominally amateur cricketers, Alfred Mynn and Nicholas Felix. The All-England XI was soon flooded with requests for fixtures from opponents offering payment because they hoped the visitors would draw a large crowd.

The team played three against-the-odds matches in 1846, taking on opponents with more than 11 players. They took on 22 of Sheffield, 18 of Manchester and 18 of Yorkshire. The matches proved a huge success.

The following season, Clarke extended the fixtures and the list of players with 'The Little Wonder' John Wisden and 'The Lion of the North' George Parr joining their ranks. Soon, the All-England XI were arranging and playing more matches than MCC.

Cricket historian Peter Wynne-Thomas wrote: 'Clarke broke through the MCC stranglehold on pukka cricket and made the sport a truly national game. He enabled the general public to see the great players of the time, and a lucky few of each locality, usually 22 young hopefuls, could actually test their cricketing ability against England's best. Local newspapers gave extensive coverage to these All-England matches, so even those who were unable to see the cricket itself could read about it.'

By 1849, the fixture list was extended to 21 matches, of which the All-England XI won 14 and lost only two. Two years later, 24 matches were contested, including four important non-odds games.

However, by 1852, storm clouds were brewing. Although the All-England XI players were better paid by Clarke than they were by MCC or the counties, the captain kept the lion's share of the profits generated by matches. Some of the professionals, notably Wisden and Jemmy Dean, were not happy with their contracts. They broke away from the team and created the United All-England XI and arranged contests with the same opponents the All-England XI were playing against.

Other similar teams appeared from the late 1850s, including the United North of England XI and the United South of England XI, which became strongly associated with W.G. Grace.

Peace talks between Clarke, Dean and Wisden failed and the latter pair resolved that they would never play for or against any team that was managed by Clarke.

In 1856, Clarke's health failed sand he managed a solitary match for the All-England XI that summer. He died in London that August with his son Alfred rushing from an All-England XI match in Loughborough but failing to make it to his father's deathbed in time.

Clarke was succeeded by his Nottinghamshire colleague Parr, who agreed that the All-England XI and United All-England XI should regularly play against each other. In 1859, six members of each team composed the squad of the first ever overseas touring English team, which played several games in the United States and in Canada (see Moment 8).

However, with the rise of county cricket and the introduction of international cricket, the travelling elevens lost influence and popularity. The All-England XI gradually faded from the scene and had disappeared by 1880.

Clarke's role as a pioneer of cricket remains undimmed. A stand still bears his name at Trent Bridge while the tours his teams undertook helped spread cricket around the world and inspired others, particularly in Australia. Australian cricketing entrepreneurs soon began arranging their own overseas tours, which went on to cement cricketing ties between England and Australia.

7

Tasmania versus Victoria *(1851)*

Launceston Racecourse, Launceston, 11–12 February 1851

Victoria	Tasmania
82	104
Philpott, Brodie 17	Du Croz 27
McDowall 5-27	Antill 7-33
57	37/7
Hamilton 35	Tabart 15
Henty 5-26	Antill 6-19

Tasmania won by three wickets

A CHALLENGE laid down to the cricketers of Van Diemen's Land from their counterparts in the Port Phillip district in 1850 marked the beginning of first-class cricket in Australia. The match took place the following year and provided a vital milestone on cricket's path from popular pastime to national sport in Australia.

Cricket had been played in Australia from soon after the first European settlers arrived and the colonies established. References to cricket can be found in the Sydney newspapers as early as 1804 while the game was gaining in popularity in Tasmania by the 1810s with the island's first recorded matches taking place in 1825.

The Melbourne Cricket Club (MCC) was formed in 1838, only three years after the founding of the city of Melbourne. The MCC would go on to play a key role in Australian cricket for the rest of the century and far beyond.

The match was the idea of MCC member William Philpott, who proposed that a cricketing challenge be sent to Launceston for a match between teams representing Port Phillip and Van Diemen's Land.

Although the proposal was made in January 1850 the match took over 12 months to arrange, due to the slow speed of communications prevalent at the time. In the interim legislation was passed in the UK Parliament to separate the Port Phillip District, which was to be renamed as Victoria, from the colony of New South Wales.

Two weeks of celebrations were arranged to mark Victoria's independence and the match was scheduled to be part of the festivities in February 1851.

The match, which was the first Australian intercolonial match, was played at the Launceston Racecourse over two days.

The visitors were drawn exclusively from the MCC and were now representing the new colony of Victoria. They were captained by Philpott and expected to win the match as their bowlers used the faster overarm technique and cricket was generally regarded as more advanced on mainland Australia.

The Van Diemen's Land team, which was commonly called Tasmania by the newspapers of the day, was made up of players from both Launceston and Hobart cricket clubs. Underarm bowling was still the prevalent technique in Tasmania at the time.

The pitch at the Launceston Racecourse ground was in a poor state; it looked difficult for batting and the umpires were unsure where best to set up the wickets. The Victoria team were unhappy with the state of the pitch and would later receive an apology from the government of Tasmania.

The match began on 11 February and was scheduled to be played to a finish with no time limit. Overs comprised four deliveries and there was no set boundary, so runs could only be scored by running between the wickets, and not by hitting fours or sixes.

Tasmania's captain John Marshall won the toss and put Victoria in to bat in front of around 1,000 spectators, who had not been charged for admission.

Philpott opened the batting for Victoria and was joint-top scorer in their first innings with 17, a score matched by James Brodie. The Victorians struggled to adapt to the pitch and the slow pace of the underarm bowling and were all out for 82 in 26 overs. Tasmania only used two bowlers with Robert McDowall taking 5-27 and William Henty 4-52 with Victoria's Charles Lister run out.

In reply, Tasmania scored 104 despite the efforts of Thomas Antill who took three wickets in four balls at one stage of the innings as he returned figures of 7-33. Opener Gervase Du Croz top-scored for the home side with 27 while captain Marshall added 13. Only two other batsmen reached double figures but crucially Victoria conceded 24 extras.

Victoria's second innings was saved by Thomas Hamilton's 35, which was the top score for the whole match. No other batsman reached double figures as the visitors were all out for 57 the second time round, leaving Tasmania a target of 36 runs to win.

Although it was getting late on the first day, the home side began their second innings. However, by the time the umpires called off play due to bad light they had been reduced to 15/6, still 21 runs short of victory.

John Tabart was unbeaten overnight and his 15 was vital in seeing Tasmania get home early on the second day for the loss of only one further wicket. Antill took another six wickets in the innings to finish with match figures of 13-52.

The match sparked an interest in intercolonial cricket in Australia and it spread over the following years. In 1852, a team from Tasmania travelled to Victoria for a return match and were defeated by 61 runs. A deciding game was played in Launceston in 1854 with Tasmania winning under the captaincy of Marshall, who was 58 years old at the time.

Elsewhere, Victoria began playing against New South Wales, who also played matches against Queensland while Norwood Cricket Club in Adelaide arranged games against Melbourne.

The 1851 match was later designated as the inaugural first-class match to be played in Australia. It boosted the popularity of cricket in Australia and ensured that when England teams began touring in the 1860s they were met enthusiastically. Those matches led to an increase in the playing skill of Australian cricketers and ultimately the formation of a national Australia side.

8

The first overseas tour *(1859)*

THE TOUR of North America undertaken by George Parr's XI in 1859 was a true landmark, not only in cricket, but sport. Not only was it the first overseas cricket tour but it both pre-dated, and inspired, rugby tours and took place 13 years before the first ever football international.

'In the year 1859 cricket entered upon its last, or oceanic stage, for at the end of the English season 12 professional cricketers crossed the Atlantic to play a short series of matches in Canada and the United States,' wrote H.S. Altham in *A History of Cricket*.

The tour was the brainchild of William Pickering, who had played cricket for Eton and Cambridge University before emigrating to Canada. Pickering opened discussions with cricketing entrepreneur Fred Lillywhite, as well as the players George Parr and John Wisden.

The English team required a guarantee of £600, which Pickering obtained through the combined efforts of Montreal Cricket Club, Hamilton Cricket Club and St George's Cricket Club.

The touring party selected could boast the pick of the All-England XI and the United All-England XI with the teams supplying half each of the 12-man squad.

It was captained by Parr, who was joined by his Nottinghamshire team-mates James Grundy and John

Jackson as well as Alfred 'Ducky' Diver and Thomas Hayward of Cambridgeshire. Surrey supplied William Caffyn, Tom Lockyer and Julius Caesar while Sussex was represented by Wisden and John Lillywhite.

Fred Lillywhite acted as tour manager, press reporter and scorer for the tour and travelled with both a pitch-side scoring booth and a printing press.

The touring party gathered at the George Hotel in Liverpool and departed for North America aboard the SS *Nova Scotian* on 7 September. After a stormy 15-day crossing of the Atlantic the tourists arrived in Canada.

The team played five matches, two in Canada and three in the United States. They also played three exhibition matches and enjoyed two excursions to Niagara Falls.

The contests were odds matches played against 22-man teams and as such did not have first-class status. However, the tourists were far too strong for the locals, as was to be expected from a team featuring the cream of England's cricketing talent and they comfortably won all of their matches.

A crowd of 3,000 turned out to see the first match in Montreal, which saw the George Parr XI triumph over Lower Canada's 22 men by eight wickets, with Parr himself taking 16 wickets during the match.

The first match of the United States leg took place on the Elysian Fields in Hoboken, New Jersey. Once again, the tourists drew a large crowd with around 25,000 spectators watching the match over three days. The English team had far too much skill for their opponents and won by an innings and 64 runs. Caffyn's bowling was almost unplayable as he took 16-25 in the second innings.

The second match against the USA team was at Philadelphia on the Camac Estate and was a closer game with the tourists winning by seven wickets.

The tour then returned to Canada where Upper Canada were beaten by ten wickets at Hamilton, Ontario. Parr put in a fine all-round performance, top-scoring with 24 in the tourists' first innings and taking 16 wickets in the match.

The final official match of the tour saw Parr's XI take on a combined 22 from the USA and Canada. Wisden starred with the ball, taking 29 wickets in the match, including a double hat-trick of six wickets in six balls, while Hayward hit a half-century. The result was another one-sided victory by an innings and 68 runs at Rochester, New York.

Some unscheduled exhibition matches followed, including one that was interrupted by snow, before the tourists returned home. They sailed up the St Lawrence river passing the *Nova Scotian* and signalling 'All Matches Won' on a large board. Despite a rougher passage on the way back the touring party all returned safely on 11 November.

Lillywhite recorded the tour for posterity with a book entitled *The English Cricketers' Trip to Canada and the United States*.

Financially the tour was a success with the large crowds guaranteeing a healthy profit and each member of the touring party earning around £90.

However, the growth of cricket in the US was stymied by the outbreak of the American Civil War less than two years later. The hostilities prevented a follow-up tour being arranged. Furthermore, the troops on both sides adopted the game of baseball, which became America's summer pastime.

Nevertheless, the concept of touring had been proven as viable and three years later English cricketers would make their first tour of Australia, setting in motion international cricket, Test matches and an enduring rivalry.

9

Wisden goes to press *(1864)*

THE YEAR of 1864 saw some major cricketing events. Overarm bowling was legalised, a 15-year-old W.G. Grace burst on to the scene with scores of 170 and 56 against the Gentlemen of Sussex and the first edition of *Wisden Cricketers' Almanack* was published.

Commonly known simply as *Wisden*, the little yellow book is often labelled the 'Bible of cricket' and has been published every year since 1864, including through two world wars and the Covid pandemic.

Wisden has become synonymous with cricket, thanks to its annual mix of commentary, reviews, statistics and awards. The influential 'Notes by the Editor' are eagerly awaited by many as an annual commentary on the state of the sport while to be named one of the 'Five Cricketers of the Year' is regarded as a major honour by players around the globe.

Wisden Cricketers' Almanack was founded by the cricketer John Wisden. Wisden was a bowler of some renown in the mid-19th century. Known as the 'Little Wonder', because he was only 5ft 4in tall and weighed just 7st, Wisden bowled a mixture of slow underarm and fast roundarm to great effect and was a member of William Clarke's All-England XI.

In 1850, he took ten wickets in an innings – all bowled – in a North versus South encounter at Lord's. It remains a record in first-class cricket. Nine years later he was one of the party on George Parr's pioneering tour of North America (see Moment 8).

Wisden also owned a sports equipment store in London's West End. As his cricketing career was coming to a close, he founded *The Cricketer's Almanack* (the apostrophe was moved a few years later) to help promote the store. Initially, it was a competitor to Fred Lillywhite's *The Guide to Cricketers*.

The first edition was published in 1864 and was 112 pages long – it now regularly runs to over 1,500 pages. As well as cricket, the first edition contained a list of St Leger winners, the rules of quoits, the dates of the Crusades and an account of the trial of Charles I.

In 1889, the 'Five Cricketers of the Year' feature was first published and the almanack has named the 'Leading Cricketer in the World' for the previous calendar year since 2004. Players can only feature in the 'Five Cricketers of the Year' once but can be the 'Leading Cricketer in the World' on multiple occasions. India's Virat Kohli won the award three times in a row between 2016 and 2018.

As well as the 'Notes by the Editor' there will be around a hundred pages of articles on cricketing topics and the 'Records' section is a key source of statistics about the game.

The almanack contains detailed coverage and scorecards from English, international and domestic cricket from around the world.

Throughout its history, *Wisden* has had only 16 editors. The longest-serving was Sydney Pardon, who was at the helm for 34 years between 1891 and 1925. The current editor is Lawrence Booth, who was the youngest editor for 72 years when he took the reins for the 2012 edition at the age of 35.

John Arlott, Neville Cardus and E.W. Swanton are amongst the many cricket writers who have contributed to *Wisden*, along with notable cricketers and successful people from other walks of life who have a keen interest in the game.

Wisden adopted its famous yellow cover along with its woodcut image of two Victorian gentlemen playing cricket in top hats for its 75th edition in 1938.

Throughout its history, *Wisden* has maintained its independence from any cricket administration. This jealously guarded unofficial status is vital to the book's status as the 'Bible of cricket', trusted and enjoyed by cricket fans around the world for over 150 years.

10

W.G. Grace's 'annus mirabilis' *(1871)*

THE IMPOSING figure of W.G. Grace stood over English cricket like a colossus for over 40 seasons. Yet, it was in 1871 that the 'Doctor' rewrote the record book for batting as he enjoyed what would become known as his 'annus mirabilis'.

Before the 1871 season, bowlers had enjoyed the upper hand in cricket aided and abetted by poor, unprepared pitches. After Grace's feats that summer, cricket was to become increasingly a batter's game. Both the volume of runs he scored and the manner in which he scored them helped reshape the game and laid the foundations for modern batting techniques in the process.

During the 1871 season, Grace amassed 2,739 runs – nobody had scored over 2,000 prior to this. It was a record that stood for a quarter of a century. The next-highest-run scorer in 1871 was Harry Jupp, who totalled 1,068. Grace hit 10 of the 17 first-class centuries scored that summer, with a top score of 268.

Grace's batting average was 78.25 in 1871 whereas the next-best average by a batsman playing more than a single innings was 39.57, just over half of Grace's figure. All this was achieved in a wet, windy summer when conditions were rarely ideal for batting.

Grace contributed with the ball too that season, taking 79 wickets at 17.02 with a best of 7-67. He claimed five wickets in an innings five times and twice took ten in a match.

Grace had begun his top-class cricket career in 1864 at the age of 15 and he had already established himself as the sport's outstanding player by the start of the 1871 season. That summer he would play for the newly formed Gloucestershire, Marylebone Cricket Club (MCC), the Gentlemen, and the United South of England Eleven (USEE).

The Doctor set the tone for the season in the opening fixture as his 181 for MCC against Surrey at Lord's set up victory for the home side by an innings and 23 runs. A week later, playing for MCC against Yorkshire at Lord's, he was denied a second century of the season when he was run out. However, his 98 was enough to help MCC to a 55-run victory.

He finished the month of May with another two centuries, scoring 118 for the Gentlemen of the South against their northern counterparts and 178 for the South against the North at Lord's. Grace added a fourth century in five matches on 1 June with 162 for the Gentlemen against Cambridge University. He also recorded bowling figures of 7-103 in Cambridge's second innings for good measure.

The Doctor's scores were modest for the rest of June; a 49 and 34 for Gloucestershire were followed by an 88 for MCC. His best form returned the following month and many people considered his unbeaten 189 in a Married versus Single game at Lord's as the finest innings of his career.

Despite heavy rain falling before the match rendering the wicket damp, soft and nearly unplayable, Grace carried his bat. His efforts ensured the Single team won by an innings and 73 runs.

This was followed by 51 for MCC in a low-scoring match against Kent and another century, this time in a losing cause, for the MCC against Surrey.

Playing in a North versus South match at The Oval later in the month Grace was out to Jem Shaw for a rare duck in the first innings. He atoned for this slip with the highest score of his career to that date in the second with 268.

'I puts the ball where I likes and he puts it where he likes,' a shell-shocked Shaw commented after the match.

Grace passed 2,000 runs for the season during a North versus South match in Canterbury in early August before adding another century for MCC Gentlemen against Kent. Then he played for the Gentlemen against the Players in Brighton and for the second time that summer, followed a first-innings duck with a double century. Grace and his brother Fred shared a second-wicket partnership of 241, with W.G. going on to score 217.

Although Gloucestershire lost by ten wickets to Nottinghamshire at Trent Bridge, Grace scored 79 and 116. It was the first time that anyone had scored a century on the ground and Grace's presence ensured a bumper crowd with over £400 being taken at the gate. This money went a long way towards the £1,500 that Nottinghamshire needed to build the Trent Bridge pavilion.

His final first-class match of the season was at Maidstone, where his own select team played Kent in a benefit match. The match was drawn; Grace scored 81 not out and 42 not out and took ten wickets in the match with 6-67 in the first innings and 4-83 in the second.

Although Grace had other great seasons, notably in 1876 and 1895, it was 1871 that cricket historian H.S. Altham described as his 'annus mirabilis'.

The Doctor himself described it as 'one of my best seasons', saying that he had needed to apply great patience when batting in 1871 because of the generally wet weather, which produced poor wickets and difficult batting conditions.

Moreover, 1871 was the year when Grace developed techniques that would underpin modern batting. Before him, batsmen would play either forward or back and would often make a speciality of a certain stroke. Grace incorporated both forward and back play into his repertoire of strokes, judging which to use solely on the merits of the delivery being faced.

In his *Jubilee Book of Cricket*, England batsman K.S. Ranjitsinhji wrote: 'He revolutionised cricket, turning it from an accomplishment into a science ... He turned the old one-stringed instrument into a many-chorded lyre, a wand. Until his time a man was either a back player like Carpenter or a forward player like Pilch, a hitter like E.H. Budd or a sticker like Harry Jupp. But W.G. Grace was each and all at once.'

11

The first Test match *(1877)*

Melbourne Cricket Ground, Melbourne, 15–17 March 1877
First Test

Australia	England
245	196
Bannerman 165	Jupp 63
Shaw 3-51	Midwinter 5-78
104	108
Horan 20	Selby 38
Shaw 5-38	Kendall 7-55

Australia won by 45 runs

THE FIFTH major cricketing tour by an English side to Australia arrived to find the gap between playing standards in the two countries closing fast. For the first time the home sides were ready to meet the tourists on level terms with 11 players on each team rather than odds matches.

The meeting between James Lillywhite's XI and a Combined Australia XI, a side raised between the Victoria and New South Wales authorities, ended in victory for the home team and was later recognised as the first ever Test match.

Lillywhite's tour had left England in November 1876 as a business venture. The squad was made up entirely of professionals with leading amateurs, including W.G. Grace, left at home.

This weakened the side, particularly the batting, and only 12 players were taken in order to maximise the profits for those taking part in the tour.

Early in the trip the team were challenged to an 11-a-side game by New South Wales. Although the tourists had the better of a draw in a two-day game, Victoria issued a similar challenge, which was accepted.

Before Lillywhite's team took up that challenge the tour diverted to New Zealand for six weeks in mid-January 1877.

While there, they lost wicketkeeper Ted Pooley, who ended up in a Christchurch jail after a betting scandal, so they returned to Australia with just 11 players.

The tourists took on the combined Australian XI, their 18th match of the trip, just a day after arriving back in Melbourne by sea. Travel and constant cricket were taking their toll on the players with reserve keeper, Harry Jupp, suffering from an inflammation of the eyes.

Although Jupp was not trusted to keep wicket, the lack of any reserve meant that he had to play. This proved to be a blessing as he top-scored for England in their first innings.

On the other side Australia were missing their great fast bowler Fred Spofforth. He had refused to play after falling out with the selectors over the choice of wicketkeeper.

The sides met at the Melbourne Cricket Ground (MCG) with a crowd of around 1,500 present to witness Alfred Shaw bowl the first ball in Test cricket to Charles Bannerman.

The first Test run came off the next delivery and the first Test wicket in the fourth over when Allen Hill bowled Nat Thompson. Edward Gregory suffered the indignity of the first Test duck later in the day.

Bannerman was dropped early on by Tom Armitage, the England fielder spilling a simple chance at mid-off.

Shaw dropped him twice more and Bannerman proceeded to punish England with the first Test match century. At the close, Bannerman was unbeaten and had made 126 out of a score of 166/6.

Bannerman was finally forced to retire hurt on 165 after lunch on the following day when the middle finger on his right hand was split by a lob from George Ulyett. He had scored 67 per cent of the runs in the innings, which remains a record. His score is still the highest by an Australian on their Test debut.

In reply to Australia's 245, England made 109/4 by the close of play. Jupp was on 54 not out despite dislodging a bail with his foot before he had scored. However, he was given not out and went on to make 63.

The third day's play attracted an estimated 12,000 spectators, who saw England bowled out for 196 with Billy Midwinter taking 5-78 for Australia.

Despite his injury Bannerman opened the second innings for Australia and was dropped again. This time he was unable to make England pay and was out for just 4, bowled by Ulyett.

Australia were dismissed for 104 second time around with the last-wicket partnership of Tom Kendall and John Hodges putting on 29 to extend the lead to 153.

Kendall then took 7-55 with his slow bowling as England were skittled for 108 in their second innings.

The margin of Australia's victory was 45 runs, a result famously repeated in the Centenary Test in March 1977.

The Australian captain Dave Gregory was given a gold medal by the Victorian Cricket Association, while his team-mates received silver medals. In addition, a public subscription raised £83 for Bannerman and £23 for Kendall and wicketkeeper John Blackham.

Following the success of the first Test, a second was quickly arranged, with the tourists taking a larger slice of the gate receipts. The Melbourne Cricket Club contributed £50 to the cost of bringing New South Welshmen, such as Spofforth and Billy Murdoch, down to Melbourne.

The England team performed far better in the second Test. On the first day, Australia won the toss but were bowled out for 122. In reply, England posted 261, led by Ulyett's half-century and Andrew Greenwood's 49, giving the tourists a healthy first-innings lead of 139.

Australia batted much better second time around with Gregory's 43 helping them to a total of 259, which set a victory target of 121. Ulyett scored 63 as England secured victory by four wickets on the third afternoon.

The Test matches, particularly the first one, generated much interest in the Australian press. However, there was initially little coverage in England and it was only later that any real note was taken of them there. In time the matches were recognised as the first matches played in the sport's premier format of Test cricket.

12

The birth of the Ashes *(1882)*

The Oval, London, 28–29 August 1882
Test match

Australia	England
63	101
Blackham 17	Ulyett 26
Barlow 5-19	Spofforth 7-46
122	77
Massie 55	Grace 32
Peate 4-40	Spofforth 7-44

Australia won by 7 runs

ALTHOUGH THE first Test match between England and Australia had been played five years earlier it was the birth of the Ashes in 1882 that put the seal on a rivalry that would become the most enduring in world cricket.

England had lost to Australia before, but defeat on home soil was previously unthinkable. The visitors' narrow victory at The Oval in 1882 changed that and prompted the famous mock obituary in *The Sporting Times*.

The obituary said that English cricket had died, with the body to be cremated and the ashes taken to Australia. This sparked the quest to regain the ashes, which England managed on that winter's tour down under and the two nations have been squabbling over possession of the little urn ever since.

Ashes series have given Test cricket some of its greatest, most iconic and most controversial moments. It is a rivalry that remains as intense as ever as it heads towards its 150th anniversary.

Initially, the one-off match between England and the touring Australians played at The Oval in late August 1882 wasn't even considered a Test match, although it was later granted that status. It did, however, produce one of the closest finishes ever seen in Test cricket. It was a match so tense that one spectator reportedly died while another famously chewed through the handle of his umbrella as Australia clinched a seven-run victory.

On the first morning of the match it was Australian captain Billy Murdoch who won the toss and opted to bat. That looked to be a poor decision as his team were all out for just 63 runs in a little over two hours. Only three of the Australian batsmen reached double figures as wicketkeeper Jack Blackham top-scored with 17. Murdoch scored 13 while Tom Garrett added 10 to the tourists' total as they were skittled by England.

Dick Barlow was the pick of the English bowlers, taking 5-19 to leave Australia reeling, while opening bowler Ted Peate took 4-31.

Barlow then opened the batting with W.G. Grace as England replied. Grace became the first of Fred Spofforth's 14 victims in the match when the Australian quick clean bowled him for 4 runs. Spofforth's raw pace was too much for the England batsmen to handle and in the first innings he took 7-46 from 36.3 overs, of which 18 were maidens.

George Ulyett top-scored for England in their first innings with 26 off 59 balls before becoming Spofforth's third victim while Maurice Read contributed a useful 19 not out. Barlow scored 11 and Allan Steel added 14 from nine balls as England established a first-innings lead of 38. The hosts were all out for 101 at stumps on the first day at The Oval.

The following day Australia's openers, Alick Bannerman and Hugh Massie, began their second innings by putting on 66 for the first wicket. Massie's impressive 55, which was the highest individual score of the match, was ended when he was clean bowled by Steel, triggering a mini-collapse. The tourists lost four wickets for just 13 runs as George Bonnor and Tom Horan fell cheaply while Bannerman joined his fellow opener back in the pavilion for 13.

Although the Australian skipper Murdoch steadied the ship with a vital 29 the last four wickets fell for just eight runs. This collapse was sparked by Grace's unsportsmanlike run-out of Sammy Jones, who had wandered out of his crease thinking the ball was dead. Australia had made 122 in their second innings, setting the home team an achievable target of 85 for victory.

Crucially, Grace's actions had only served to spur on the irrepressible Spofforth, who declared: 'This thing can be done.'

The home side reached 15 before Spofforth struck by clean bowling Albert 'Monkey' Hornby for 9. Barlow was castled first ball to leave Spofforth on a hat-trick but the fast bowler was unable to claim his third wicket.

Grace and Ulyett then put together a partnership of 36 before Spofforth had the latter caught behind for 11. Grace fell two runs later, caught by Bannerman off the bowling of Harry Boyle for 32 and England were reeling at 53/4. Wicketkeeper Alfred Lyttleton provided some resistance with 12 from 55 balls before he too was removed by Spofforth.

The fast bowler then cleaned up Steel and Read for ducks in the same over to leave England on 75/8, still ten runs from victory with just two wickets remaining. The very next over Boyle removed Billy Barnes for 2 and then, with the last ball of his over, clean bowled Peate to leave England 77 all out.

The home side's collapse had left them seven runs short of victory to stun The Oval crowd. However, the spectators soon recovered and rushed on to the pitch to congratulate Spofforth on his match figures of 14-90.

The press savaged the England players for losing on home soil for the first time. Two days later, on 2 September, a mock obituary, written by Reginald Brooks under the pseudonym 'Bloobs', appeared in *The Sporting Times*.

It read:

'In Affectionate Remembrance of
ENGLISH CRICKET,
which died at the Oval on 29 August 1882,
Deeply lamented by a large circle of sorrowing friends and acquaintances.

R.I.P.

N.B. – The body will be cremated and the ashes taken to Australia.'

England toured Australia the following winter with captain Ivo Bligh vowing to return home with 'the ashes' and Murdoch promising to defend them. The phrase was seized upon by the Australian press as England triumphed 2-1 in a three-match series.

After England played in a social match at the Rupertswood Estate outside Melbourne on Christmas Eve

1882 Bligh was given the small terracotta urn as a symbol of the ashes that he had travelled to Australia to regain. After his death the urn was bequeathed to MCC and it is now housed in the Lord's museum.

Since then the iconic little urn has come to represent the rivalry between two sporting nations across a number of sports. But it will always be most closely associated with the regular battles for cricket supremacy played by England and Australia before packed houses to this day.

13

South Africa joins Test cricket *(1889)*

SOUTH AFRICA'S entry into the Test cricket arena in 1889 was a significant milestone in the development of cricket as a true international sport.

England and Australia had been meeting each other regularly since they played the first Test match 12 years earlier and the Ashes rivalry was gradually taking shape. However, it was South Africa's admission to the Test-playing ranks that helped put international cricket on the road from a bilateral contest to a global game.

A team of English cricketers toured South Africa during 1888 and 1889. After playing a number of provincial games two of their matches were against a team representing all of South Africa. In 1897, it was officially decided that these should retrospectively be assigned Test match status.

These two matches were the first Test matches to include South Africa and the first of the two was also the inaugural first-class match played in the country.

Questions have been asked about the quality of both sides, as well as the standard of the pitches the matches were played on. Only five of the English team had previously played Test cricket and few of the South Africans would play internationally again. Nevertheless, the matches retain Test match status to this day and so they remain the birthplace of South Africa in international cricket.

The English team toured South Africa under the management of Major R.G. Warton, a retired British Army officer who had served in South Africa and was a member of the Western Province Cricket Club.

Cricket was growing in popularity in South Africa with both Newlands in Cape Town and the Old Wanderers in Johannesburg opening in 1888. Warton was invited to bring a team of English players to tour the country and sponsorship was secured from shipping magnate Sir Donald Currie.

Local agents made the arrangements for the tour while Warton travelled to England and recruited players. His captain was the future Hollywood actor C. Aubrey Smith, who had played for Cambridge University and Sussex.

There were five players in the touring party with Test match experience. These included spinner Johnny Briggs, who was the first man to take 100 Test wickets, George Ulyett, a veteran of the 1877 inaugural Test in Melbourne, Maurice Read, Harry Wood and Bobby Abel.

Their experience was supplemented by Monty Bowden, Arnold Fothergill and Frank Hearne, who like the captain had all played for English counties. However, Charles Coventry, Basil Grieve and Emile McMaster never played in any first-class matches aside from the two Tests on the tour. Cricket historian H.S. Altham described the team's overall standard as 'about that of a weak county'.

Warton's XI played 20 matches on the tour but only the two Test matches were recognised as first-class games. The other matches were either too short – a first-class match must be scheduled for at least three days – or played against odds. When playing against the odds the tourists fielded 11 players while the home teams would field between 15 and 22 players.

Warton's XI met sides from four of the South African provinces: Eastern Province, Natal, Transvaal and Western Province. They also played teams representing the cities of Cape Town, Durban, Johannesburg, Kimberley, Pietermaritzburg and Port Elizabeth.

Although the tour got off to a poor start with the team losing four of their opening six fixtures, they comfortably won both matches against the South African XI.

The first Test started on 12 March 1889 and was played in Port Elizabeth with around 3,000 spectators present on the first day. South Africa's captain Owen Dunell won the toss and chose to bat on the green matting pitch.

The pitch was not easy for batting and the South Africans were all out for 84, which was scored at a glacial pace from 75.2 overs. Two batsmen accounted for well over half the runs as Bernard Tancred top-scored with 29 while Dunell finished unbeaten on 26. England's captain Smith took 5-19 while Briggs took 4-39.

Abel led England's response with 46 as the tourists were bowled out for 148 in their reply. South Africa made a better fist of their second innings with Tancred once again leading the way with another 29. The hosts were all out for 129 to set the tourists a target of 66 for victory.

England duly knocked off the target in the 22nd over with Abel finishing on 23 not out and Ulyett contributing 22 as they sealed victory late on the second day.

The two sides met again at Newlands 12 days later and the result was a far more comprehensive victory for England. Smith was ill with a fever and so Bowden became England's youngest ever Test captain, aged 23 years and 144 days.

Bowden won the toss and chose to bat with England racking up a formidable 292 in their first innings. Abel starred again with a century. His score of 120 would have ultimately been enough to win the match on its own as South Africa were twice knocked over cheaply at the hands of Briggs.

The Lancashire spinner took seven wickets in the first innings, which was notable for Tancred becoming the first Test player to ever carry his bat as he finished unbeaten on 26. Despite the opener's efforts his side were all out for 47 and forced to follow on.

Briggs took another eight wickets in the second innings, all bowled, to finish with match figures of 15-28. South Africa were all out for 43 as England cruised to an innings-and-202-run victory in Cape Town.

Despite the two Test defeats and the fact the tour did not make a profit, first-class cricket in South Africa was provided with a huge boost.

Currie, who had sponsored the tour, was so impressed that he decided to donate the trophy named after him, the Currie Cup, as the prize for winning South Africa's domestic championship each year.

For the 1888/89 season, the English team were asked to award the cup to the team which had excelled most against them – they chose Kimberley. In 1889/90, the competition proper began with a challenge by Transvaal to Kimberley.

South Africa made a slow start to life as a Test team, losing ten and drawing one of their first 11 matches. However, by early in the 20th century they were emerging as a side that could regularly challenge and beat England and Australia. The Test cricket club had a third member and the door was now open for further nations to join.

14

The County Championship gets underway *(1890)*

THE OPENING play of the first County Championship saw W.G. Grace face Bobby Peel as Gloucestershire took on Yorkshire in Bristol on 12 May 1890. Later that day, the home side's James Cranston went on to score the new competition's first century. However, it was Yorkshire who went on to claim the first victory with an eight-wicket win that was sealed on the third afternoon of play.

The inaugural season of the County Championship was played between eight counties – Nottinghamshire, Surrey, Lancashire, Kent, Middlesex, Gloucestershire, Yorkshire and Sussex. The final positions in 1890 were based on number of wins minus the number of losses and it was Surrey who claimed the first County Championship crown.

The first season launched the longest continuously played first-class domestic tournament in the world. The first ever Currie Cup match had been played a month earlier in South Africa. However, that competition was sporadic in its early years whereas only the two World Wars and the Covid-19 pandemic have prevented the County Championship from being completed every year since 1890.

The English counties had been playing each other long before the Championship was officially launched, with the first known match taking place between Kent and Surrey in 1709. During the 18th century such matches grew in popularity, although the counties themselves were often represented by their pre-eminent club side in the area.

This saw Dartford playing on behalf of Kent, Hambledon for Hampshire and Slindon representing Sussex while London often played against county teams and was regarded by many as another county club.

The most successful county teams of the era were Hampshire, Kent, Middlesex, Surrey and Sussex. The best team was often acknowledged by the opportunity to play against an All-England XI.

The following century saw the formation of the county cricket clubs that we would recognise today. The existing counties were joined by Nottinghamshire, Lancashire, Middlesex and Yorkshire. As the popularity of cricket continued to grow throughout the century there was more and more interest in which club could claim to be the champion county.

However, fixture lists were erratic with different counties playing differing numbers of matches and facing different sets of opponents during the season. Until 1864 the title was simply claimed by, or accorded to, a particular team, but it was far from definitive.

Nevertheless, there were periods of dominance achieved by certain counties over a number of years including Kent in the 1720s, Hampshire in the 1770s and 1780s, Sussex in the 1820s and Surrey in the 1850s.

Between 1864 and the start of the official Championship in 1890 a consensus began to grow from the cricketing press, including *Wisden*, and expert cricketers, such as W.G. Grace, as to who were the champion county. During this period, it was the turn of Nottinghamshire to dominate as they collected eight titles and shared a further seven.

During the 1870s newspapers had begun to print tables of inter-county results and then declare a champion on the basis of their chosen criteria. However, as the decade wore on it became widely accepted that the side with fewest losses should be the champions. Meanwhile, the clamour for a form of league system, which would give a conclusive champion county, continued to grow.

When the annual meeting of county club secretaries was held at Lord's on 10 December 1889, their purpose was to decide on a fixture programme for the 1890 season.

Cricket: A Weekly Record of the Game reported: 'While the secretaries were engaged in making the fixtures the representatives of the eight leading counties – Nottinghamshire, Surrey, Lancashire, Kent, Middlesex, Gloucestershire, Yorkshire, and Sussex – held a private meeting to discuss the method by which the county championship should in future be decided.

'The meeting was, we understand, not quite unanimous, but a majority were in favour of ignoring drawn games altogether and settling the question of championship by wins and losses. As it was agreed to abide by the views of the majority, this decision was accepted as final.

'Subsequently representatives of the following eight minor counties – Derbyshire, Warwickshire, Leicestershire, Hampshire, Somersetshire, Staffordshire, Durham and Essex – held a similar meeting in private, and unanimously decided to apply the same rule to minor county cricket.'

The original eight teams were joined by Somerset in the second season of the Championship and 1895 saw the addition of Derbyshire, Essex, Hampshire, Leicestershire and Warwickshire.

Since then, four more counties have been added – Worcestershire, Northamptonshire, Glamorgan and

Durham – to take the total to the present day 18 participants. In 2000, the counties were split into two divisions and a system of promotion and relegation was introduced.

1895 also saw the first of many changes to the points system, which was modified so that the ratio of points to finished games (games minus draws) decided the final positions.

In 1910, the system was modified again, so that the order was based on ratio of matches won to matches played, while from 1911 to 1967 a variety of systems were used that generally relied on points for wins and for first-innings leads in games left unfinished.

Since 1968, the basis has been wins and 'bonus points', which are earned for scoring a certain number of runs or taking a certain number of wickets in the first 110 overs of each first innings.

The 1960s also saw the entry of foreign players, which has enabled some of the finest talent ever to grace the game to take part in county cricket (see Moment 26). West Indian all-rounder Garry Sobers was among the first cohort of global stars to play for a county and those who have followed in his footsteps include Viv Richards, Sachin Tendulkar, Imran Khan, Shane Warne, Allan Border, Muttiah Muralitharan, Brian Lara, Richard Hadlee and Curtly Ambrose to name but a few.

Between them, Yorkshire and Surrey won 12 of the first 13 Championships and they remain the leading counties with the former having it 32 times outright.

15

The googly puts batsmen in a spin
(1903)

THE GOOGLY'S rise from relative obscurity to a major weapon in a leg-spinner's arsenal bamboozled batsmen in the early part of the 20th century. Its impact led to claims that the delivery was somehow unfair and against the spirit of cricket.

The googly's effectiveness stems from its deceptiveness. It is a delivery bowled by a right-arm leg-spinner. When bowled, it appears to be a leg break, but after pitching the ball turns in the opposite direction to that expected, behaving as an off break instead.

The googly is also known as the wrong'un, Bosie or Bosey, with the latter two terms referring to the man commonly credited with inventing the delivery, England's Bernard Bosanquet.

In the 1926 *Wisden Almanack*, Bosanquet wrote: 'What is the googly? It is merely a ball with an ordinary break produced by an extraordinary method. It is quite possible and, in fact, not difficult, to detect, and, once detected, there is no reason why it should not be treated as an ordinary break-back.

'The googly after all (bowled by a right-handed bowler to a right-handed batsman) is nothing more nor less than an ordinary off-break. The method of delivery is the secret of its difficulty, and this merely consisted in turning the wrist over at the moment of delivery far enough to alter the axis of spin, so that a ball which normally delivered would break from leg breaks from the off. That is all there is to it.

'From the moment it became generally recognised that a ball could be bowled which left the batsman in doubt as to which way it would break, the fun began.'

Although Bosanquet is often credited with inventing the googly, others had tried similar deliveries before him. Herbert Page of Gloucestershire is recorded as having bowled googlies in 1885 – although not in anger – while Alan Steel is believed to have sent down a googly in England's first home Test in 1880. Meanwhile, in Australia George Palmer developed a mystery ball that many equated to a googly.

However, it was Bosanquet's purple patch over the 1903 and 1904 seasons that saw the googly finally make its mark on the world of cricket and put batsmen into a spin.

The seeds of the googly were sown while Bosanquet was at Oxford University in the 1890s. There he often played a table-top game called Twisti-Twosti. The object was to bounce a tennis ball on a table so that it could not be caught by an opposing player. Bosanquet began to experiment with ways of throwing the ball so that, after pitching, it turned and spun in an unexpected direction, without his opponent detecting any difference in the delivery.

As a student, he made several appearances for Middlesex as a medium-fast bowler, but decided that he would be better rewarded if he changed to spin and mastered his mystery delivery.

It took a few years of practice with mixed results before he achieved some success. The first victim of the new delivery was Leicestershire's Samuel Coe, who was stumped after missing a googly that bounced four times before reaching the wicketkeeper.

On a tour of Australia during 1903 he took 6-153 against New South Wales, including the wicket of the great Victor Trumper with a delivery that Bosanquet claimed was the first googly ever bowled in the country.

On his return to England, Bosanquet had his best year yet with the ball in county cricket, taking 63 wickets at an average of 21.00. Although a modest return, the manner in which he bowled and took the wickets was raising eyebrows. He lacked control of his length, which limited the effectiveness of his leg breaks and googlies but he was causing batsmen problems.

Bosanquet wrote: 'I found that batsmen who used to grin at the sight of me and grasp their bat firmly by the long handle, began to show a marked preference for the other end!'

His performances were enough to earn him a place in Pelham Warner's England team to tour Australia that winter. Warner was also Bosanquet's captain at Middlesex and the selection came in for some criticism.

However, C.B. Fry wrote an open letter to Warner urging him to 'persuade that Bosanquet of yours to practise, practise, practise those funny googlies of his till he is automatically certain of his length. That leg break of his which breaks from the off might win a Test match.'

This prediction was proved accurate in the crucial fourth Test of the series. Bosanquet took 6-51 in the second innings as England won by 157 runs to take an unassailable 3-1 lead in the Ashes.

Wisden said: 'Bosanquet's value with the ball cannot be judged from the averages, as on his bad days he is, as everyone knows, one of the most expensive of living bowlers. When he was in form the Australians thought him far more difficult on hard wickets than any of the other bowlers, Clement Hill saying, without any qualification, that his presence in the eleven won the rubber.'

The 1904 season was Bosanquet's best with bat and ball. In all first-class matches, he achieved the double of 1,000 runs and 100 wickets: he scored 1,405 runs at an average of 36.02 and took 132 wickets at an average of 21.62, the only time in his career he passed 100 wickets in a season. His performance earned him selection as one of *Wisden's* Cricketers of the Year.

The following year his career as a bowler went into decline, although Bosanquet did take his Test best figures of 8-107 in 1905. After 1905, he rarely bowled and never bowled a googly, taking only 22 wickets in eight seasons.

However, there were plenty of other spinners attempting to emulate his success with the googly and putting doubt into the minds of batsmen. One of those was Bosanquet's Middlesex team-mate Reggie Schwarz, who was South African.

Schwarz in turn passed it on to the South African bowlers Aubrey Faulkner, Bert Vogler and Gordon White. These four together raised the art of bowling the googly to a high standard, becoming the first great spinning quartet in Test cricket history.

The googly was here to stay, despite the complaints of batsmen that would be passed down through the cricketing generations.

Bosanquet wrote: 'It is not for me to defend it. Other and more capable hands have taken it up and exploited it, and, if blame is to be allotted, let it be on their shoulders. For me it is the task of the historian, and if I appear too much in the role of the proud parent, I ask forgiveness.'

16

West Indies' first Test heralds new era *(1928)*

THE ENTRY of the West Indies into the Test arena in 1928 heralded a new era for international cricket. It kick-started a period that saw the number of nations playing at the top level quickly double from three to six as New Zealand and India both joined the fray within the next four years.

The three countries had been invited to attend the Imperial Cricket Conference – forerunner of the International Cricket Council – in 1926. The West Indies, New Zealand and India were all then asked to organise themselves into cricket boards that could, in future, select representative teams to take part in Test matches.

The West Indies were the first of the trio to play a Test match when they toured England two years later. The tour received vital backing from the cricket authorities due to the success of the West Indian tour to England in 1923 when the side won six first-class matches and impressed many observers.

Seven players from the 1923 touring party returned to England five years later. The team was captained by Jamaica's Karl Nunes, who had been vice-captain of the 1923 touring side. Nunes was also a part-time wicketkeeper but served as the main gloveman on the tour as no specialist had been selected.

Also returning were George Challenor of Barbados, who had been the star batsman in 1923, scoring six centuries and recording a high score of 155 as he averaged over 50 with the bat. However, he was unable to repeat this success in 1928 as his average fell to 27.53 and he failed to score a first-class century on the tour.

Trinidad & Tobago all-rounder Learie Constantine, who had been lauded for his fielding in 1923, was the visitors' star performer on the tour. He scored the most first-class runs, with 1,381 at an average of 34.52, took the most first-class wickets, with 107 at 22.95, and was the only player to score three centuries in the first-class matches.

Nevertheless, Constantine and his team-mates all struggled in the Test matches and England took the series comfortably 3-0, winning all three matches by an innings.

The West Indies were given the honour of a match at Lord's for their inaugural Test, against England. Although Constantine took 4-82 England racked up 401 in their first innings with Ernest Tyldesley scoring 122 for the hosts.

In reply, Challenor and Frank Martin put on 86 but the former's wicket sparked a batting collapse as five batsmen perished for just 10 runs. Martin scored 44 and Nunes added 37 but the West Indies were all out for 177 and were asked to follow on. Second time around the tourists were all out for 166 as England clinched victory by an innings and 58 runs early on the third day.

The second Test at Old Trafford was similarly one-sided despite the West Indies winning the toss and batting first. England spinner Tich Freeman took five wickets as the tourists were all out for 206 with another batting collapse undermining a solid start from the openers.

Douglas Jardine led the reply with 83 as England scored 351 to take a healthy first-innings lead. The lead proved to be more than enough as the West Indies never recovered from a poor start in their second innings with Freeman taking another five wickets. The tourists were all out for 115, giving England a win by an innings and 30 runs and an unassailable 2-0 lead in the series.

The third Test at The Oval followed a similar pattern to the second. The West Indians made a good start through their openers, with Clifford Roach scoring a second half-century in two matches and Challenor adding 46. However, no other batsman scored over 30 and although the total of 238 was the tourists' highest of the series it would prove to be below par.

In reply, Jack Hobbs and Herbert Sutcliffe shared a stand of over 150 as the former top-scored with 159. Herman Griffith took 6-103, the best figures of the series for the West Indies, but despite his efforts the tail wagged and the last three wickets made 105 runs to leave England all out for 438.

The West Indies' second innings, as in the previous Tests, began badly and only a stubborn 41 from Frank Martin enabled the side to reach three figures. The tourists were all out for 129 as the match was over before lunch on the third day. Victory by an innings and 71 runs clinched a comprehensive 3-0 win for the hosts.

Wisden's verdict was harsh, it said: 'So far from improving upon the form of their predecessors, the team of 1928 fell so much below it that everybody was compelled to realise that the playing of Test matches between England and West Indies was a mistake. Whatever the future may have in store, the time is certainly not yet when the West Indies can challenge England with a reasonable hope of success.'

However, these words proved to be overly pessimistic. The Marylebone Cricket Club (MCC) agreed to send a side to the West Indies for four Test matches in 1929/30. This tour coincided with a second tour to New Zealand, where the first Test matches against that country were played.

A weakened England side toured the West Indies and the series finished honours even at 1-1. It also saw the emergence of George Headley as the first great West Indian batting star.

Despite the one-sided result the entry of West Indies into Test cricket in 1928 marked the beginning of a new, global era in the sport as three key protagonists were added to the ranks of the international game. In the years to come all would make a profound impact producing star players and famous teams as they added their own chapters to cricket's rich history.

17

Records, England and the Ashes fall to Bradman *(1930)*

DON BRADMAN began Australia's 1930 Ashes tour of England as a promising young batsman and ended it as a cricketing colossus.

Although Bradman had already started down the path to greatness with some formidable scoring feats in Australia, questions were still being asked of his technique. In England those questions were answered in unequivocal terms as The Don began his domination of the cricketing world.

Bradman shattered many batting records in 1930, helping Australia regain the Ashes by beating England 2-1 in the process. He had made his Test debut two years earlier in a series that England had dominated 4-1 in Australia. An inauspicious start had seen scores of 18 and 1 at Brisbane. Despite being dropped for the second Test of the series, Bradman bounced back with centuries in the third and fifth Tests.

Although these scores showed Bradman's undoubted talent, some still had reservations that his technique would survive a thorough examination on English pitches.

Famously, England and Surrey all-rounder, Percy Fender, wrote: 'He will always be in the category of the brilliant, if unsound, ones.

'Promise there is in Bradman in plenty, though watching him does not inspire one with any confidence that he desires to take the only course which will lead him to a fulfilment of that promise.

'He makes a mistake, then makes it again and again; he does not correct it, or look as if he were trying to do so. He seems to live for the exuberance of the moment.'

If there were doubts about Bradman's technique, there were none regarding his form before he left Australia on the 1930 tour. In a trial match to select the tourists, Bradman scored 124 and 225. Against Queensland at the Sydney Cricket Ground, Bradman set a then world record for first-class cricket by scoring 452 not out. Overall, he averaged 113.28 during the 1929/30 Australian season.

The journey to England did not interrupt the flow of runs as Bradman began the tour with a double century at Worcester and 185 at Leicester. A mere 78 against Yorkshire was followed by his second double century of the tour, 252 against Surrey. A third almost followed against Hampshire and although he fell just short with 191, that was enough to have scored 1,000 runs before the end of May. Bradman was only the fifth player, and first Australian, to achieve this rare feat in England.

However, England remained the favourites for the Ashes series and enjoyed the best of the conditions in the first Test at Trent Bridge. The home side won by 93 runs, despite Bradman hitting 131 in the second innings, as Australia's run chase fell short.

The second Test at Lord's saw Bradman score 254 in an innings he himself rated as the best of his career. England had batted first and scored 425 with K.S. Duleepsinhji scoring 173. However, Bradman's double century, the highest individual score against England at the time, propelled Australia to 729/6 declared, after he shared huge stands with captain Bill Woodfull and Alan Kippax.

Wisden praised his performance for its style, power and accuracy, noting that no fault could be found with a display that gave nothing approaching a chance.

Australian leg-spinner Clarrie Grimmett then took six wickets to help bowl England out for 375 before the tourists chased down 72 to win by seven wickets and level the series.

The match proved a watershed in Ashes history. From the summer of 1926, Australia had won just one Test and lost six to England. From the Lord's Test until Bradman's retirement in 1948, the two countries would play 33 Tests of which Australia would win 16 and lose just eight.

In the third Test, at Headingley, Bradman scored a century before lunch on the first day of the match to equal the performances of his Australian predecessors Victor Trumper and Charlie Macartney. In the afternoon, Bradman added another century between lunch and tea, before finishing the day on 309 not out. He remains the only Test player to pass 300 in a single day's play. His eventual score of 334 was a world record, beating the previous mark of 325 scored by England's Andy Sandham against the West Indies, and accounted for over half of Australia's total of 566.

A Wally Hammond century helped England to escape Leeds with a draw and the fourth Test at Old Trafford also ended in a stalemate after more than a day was lost to rain. Bradman was only able to score 14 in Australia's innings, which ended his run of four consecutive Tests with a century.

The series was decided at The Oval where England batted first and scored 405 before Australia struck back, Bradman scoring another double century with 232 of the tourists' total of 695. Percy Hornibrook then took seven wickets as England were all out for 251 and Australia sealed victory by an innings and 39 runs to regain the Ashes.

The numbers achieved by Bradman on the 1930 Ashes tour tell a remarkable story. He scored 974 runs at an average of 139.14 during the Test series, with four centuries, including two double hundreds and a triple. As of 2022, no other batter has matched or exceeded 974 runs or three double centuries in one Test series; the record of 974 runs exceeds the second-best performance by 69 runs and was achieved in two fewer innings.

Over the course of the tour Bradman scored 2,960 runs at an average of 98.66 with ten centuries. This remains the most by any overseas batsman on a tour of England. During the year he had also broken the highest scores in first-class and Test matches.

Unsurprisingly, Bradman was one of *Wisden's* Cricketers of the Year. The almanack said he stood alone as a run-getter and predicted that there would be no limit to his possibilities.

Those words proved to be accurate as Bradman's exploits on the 1930 tour set in motion a period of Australian dominance in the Ashes and made him a national hero in Australia. His achievements against England came against a backdrop of the depression of the 1930s and the prodigious run-scoring of the 'Boy from Bowral' provided welcome relief for a public looking for hope despite the economic woes of the time.

18

Bodyline *(1932/33)*

THE FIERCE cricketing rivalry between England and Australia boiled over during the infamous Bodyline series of 1932/33. Tempers flared on and off the pitch, batsmen in the firing line were hurt and injured and there was almost a diplomatic incident between the two countries.

In the end order was restored and although England won the series 4-1 to regain the Ashes, their tactics on the tour led to changes to the Laws of Cricket. England's key fast bowler Harold Larwood would never play Test cricket again after the series, while the captain Douglas Jardine hardly featured, despite his success.

Jardine had been tasked with regaining the Ashes after the 1930 series in England when batting phenomenon Don Bradman had dominated the home bowling. Australia had reclaimed the little urn with a 2-1 victory with Bradman averaging an incredible 139.14 over the series, scoring 974 runs, including a world record triple century in Leeds.

The Marylebone Cricket Club (MCC) appointed Jardine to captain the following tour of Australia with a mission to stem the tide of runs and win back the Ashes. He believed Bradman struggled against balls which bounced into his chest and formed a tactic to exploit this.

The plan relied on a fearsome fast bowling unit, spearheaded by the lightning quick Larwood, who opened the bowling alongside his Nottinghamshire team-mate Bill Voce. The Notts pair were supplemented by Yorkshire's Bill Bowes and Middlesex's Gubby Allen.

Jardine said: 'The Australian batting is strong and Bradman must be dealt with if he is not to win matches by himself but they are not accustomed to, nor do they relish, real pace. I have four fast bowlers and it is they who will have to win this rubber for me. How can I best exploit their pace and at the same time conserve their energy?'

The answer to this conundrum lay in leg theory, Jardine concluded. Leg theory saw right-arm fast bowlers deliver the ball around the wicket into the batsman's body. The ball is short-pitched and the aim is to intimidate the batter and to get them to fend off the delivery towards a packed leg-side field of close catchers.

The theory originated from the end of the 19th century, when a number of bowlers began to use leg theory as a legitimate tactic.

The deliveries weren't necessarily short but the bowler would often direct the ball at, or outside of, leg stump. This made it difficult for the batsman to play a shot anywhere but on the leg side. That leg side would be packed with fielders and the aim for the bowling team was for the batters to hit the ball in their direction.

Leg theory evolved into bodyline during the 1920s with more balls directed at the batsman's body. The batsman had three choices: to move but risk exposing his wicket, to play the ball with his bat and face being caught by a ring of close fielders, or try to duck and risk painful blows.

This tactic divided opinion and when England used it extensively on the 1932/33 Ashes tour the issue exploded. The tactics were first employed in a tour match against an Australian XI in Melbourne in November and were used in earnest the following month in the first Test in Sydney.

Australia, who were without Bradman, were beaten by ten wickets. Larwood took ten wickets for the cost of 124 runs in the match while Voce chipped in with another six. Australia's batsmen were unable to cope with the pace and accuracy of England's attack with only Stan McCabe's first-innings 187 providing any real resistance.

However, claims that the Australian batsmen were being physically targeted prompted complaints from the local press and cricket fans.

Australia levelled the series with a 11-run victory in the second Test in Melbourne. Bradman returned to the side with a surprise golden duck in the first innings but made a crucial century in the second to set up the home side's win.

The win came at a physical cost for the Australian batsmen who had little to protect them from the short-pitched barrage. They were punished with repeated blows to bodies and even Bradman looked unsettled at the crease.

Feelings were running so high in the build-up to the third Test in Adelaide that the public were shut out of the ground while England practised. Matters reached fever pitch when the match began as Australians Bill Woodfull and Bert Oldfield were hurt by the bowling.

Wisden would later call it, 'probably the most unpleasant Test ever played ... altogether the whole atmosphere was a disgrace to cricket'.

Australia were replying after England had recovered from a poor start to post 341 when Woodfull misjudged a ball from Larwood. Expecting a bouncer, the Australian captain ducked and was struck above the heart.

The booing lasted for three minutes, despite the fact England had not yet deployed Bodyline tactics in the match.

That would change though, moments later, when Jardine called out to Larwood: 'Well bowled, Harold.' He then packed the leg-side field and police had to be deployed on the boundary. The next day, Oldfield had his skull cracked by Larwood, who had to be escorted from the ground.

At the end of the day's play England's tour manager Pelham Warner visited the Australian changing room on a peace mission only to be told by Woodfull: 'I don't want to see you, Mr Warner. There are two teams out there. One is trying to play cricket and the other is not.'

That comment was leaked to the press and the following day the Australian Board of Control for International Cricket sent a cable to the MCC in London.

It read: 'Bodyline bowling assumed such proportions as to menace best interests of game, making protection of body by batsmen the main consideration. Causing intensely bitter feeling between players as well as injury. In our opinion is unsportsmanlike. Unless stopped at once likely to upset friendly relations existing between Australia and England.'

The MCC replied saying that they 'deplored' the cable and the use of the term 'unsportsmanlike'. For a time, it looked as if the remainder of the tour was in doubt as Jardine made his feelings known. If the Australian board did not withdraw the accusation of unsporting behaviour, his team would not play the fourth Test.

The Australian government were concerned that sporting matters could impact on trade between the two countries and intervened. Australian Prime Minister Joseph Lyons told his country's cricket board that a British boycott of Australian goods could cripple the country. This led to the accusation of unsportsmanlike play being withdrawn, but on the understanding that Bodyline bowling would later be looked at in an official capacity as 'not in the best interests of cricket'.

The Test series continued and England won 4-1 with Bradman's batting average reduced to 56, excellent by most standards but some way below that achieved during the rest of his career.

The repercussions continued after the tour though, with ill feeling continuing for some time.

Larwood was asked to write an apology letter and he refused, so he never played Test cricket again after 1933. Jardine's final Test came a year later in 1934 but his reputation suffered a terrible blow.

Shortly after the Ashes series, a ruling was put in place stating that no more than two fielders could be placed behind square on the leg side – this curbed what had been a key tactic for Jardine's men.

The MCC also stated that Bodyline breached the spirit of the game and the English side was widely criticised within the sport.

Wisden concluded: 'Suffice to say here that a method of bowling was evolved – mainly with the idea of curbing the scoring propensities of Bradman – which met with almost general condemnation among Australian cricketers and spectators and which, when something of the real truth was ultimately known in this country, caused people at home – many of them famous in the game – to wonder if the winning of the rubber was, after all, worth this strife.'

19

The first women's Test match *(1934)*

Exhibition Ground, Brisbane, 28–31 December 1934
First Test

Australia	England
47	154
Smith 25	MacLagan 72
MacLagan 7-10	Palmer 7-18
138	34/1
Shevill 63	Snowball 18
Spear 5-15	Antonio 1-20

England won by nine wickets

THE FIRST women's Test match was played between England and Australia in 1934. The two sides met in Brisbane and the visitors won a three-day match by nine wickets.

It had been a long road for women's cricket to reach this point. The first record of a women's match taking place is in a 1745 report in the *Reading Mercury*. The newspaper covered a match in the south of England, 'between eleven maids of Bramley and eleven maids of Hambleton'.

In Australia, the Siroccos met the Fernleas in front of more than 1,000 spectators at the Sydney Cricket Ground in 1886, while a year later back in England, the White Heather Club, the first women's club, was established.

Finally, as opportunities for women slowly opened up following World War One, the Women's Cricket

Association was founded in England in 1926. Five years later the Australia Women's Cricket Council came into being and they issued an invitation for the England women to tour Australia and New Zealand.

Even then, the criteria for the touring party was strict. Players had to contribute £80 for the six-month trip while married women were not considered for the tour. This ruled out some players who should have been guaranteed a place in the team.

Players also had to agree not to smoke, drink or gamble or 'be accompanied by a man'. In the end seven teachers, two secretaries, two art students, a lawyer, an army auxiliary and two ladies of leisure, set sail from Tilbury docks in October 1934.

Despite being understrength, England proved too good for their hosts and they remained unbeaten on the tour.

In the first Test in Brisbane, England bundled the Australians out for just 47 with Myrtle MacLagan taking 7-10 in 17 overs. Kath Smith's 25 was the only double-digit score as the home side suffered four ducks in the innings.

MacLagan then scored the first half-century in women's Tests with a 72 that underpinned England's reply. The tourists amassed a lead of 107 runs after being bowled out for 154 on the second day of the match. Australia's Annie Palmer was the pick of the home bowlers as she took 7-18 in 13.2 overs.

By the end of the second day, Australia had lost half their side for 99 in the second innings. The rest day failed to benefit the Australians with only Essie Shevill's unbeaten 63 providing any resistance as they subsided to 138 all out. A target of just 32 runs did not present a challenge to England, who cruised home in less than 13 overs with nine wickets to spare.

England also won the second Test, with Australia grinding out an improved first-innings total of 162, which included a 47-minute duck for Shevill. Smith again top-scored, this time with 47.

England responded with a formidable innings of 301/5 declared. MacLagan and Betty Snowball put on 149 for the first wicket and the former went on to make the first century in women's Tests.

Joy Partridge then took 6-96 as Australia reached 149 second time around. Although this was enough to make England bat again, the target of 10 was knocked off in six overs to give the tourists a 2-0 lead in the series.

The third Test, in Melbourne, was a draw – MacLagan making 50 and taking seven match wickets – as Australia improved fast.

The tour moved on to New Zealand where the one Test match saw England romp to victory by an innings and 337 runs after big centuries by Snowball and Molly Hide.

In total, England won eight, drew four and lost none with two matches abandoned on the tour.

However, two years later a much-improved Australia team toured England and a three-Test series ended 1-1 after some close finishes to the matches.

20

Time is called on the timeless Test
(1939)

Kingsmead, Durban, 3–14 March 1939

South Africa	England
530	316
Pieter van der Bijl 125	Les Ames 84
Reg Perks 5-100	Eric Dalton 4-59
481	654/5
Alan Melville 103	Bill Edrich 219
Ken Farnes 4-74	Eric Dalton 2-100

Match drawn

THE LAST timeless Test match was played between England and South Africa in 1939. The match was abandoned as a draw after ten days of play, spread over 12 calendar days, because the England touring party had to catch their boat home.

The match set a number of records including most days played in a Test and most balls bowled with 5,447. In addition, England's second-innings total for 654/5 is the highest fourth-innings total in a Test match.

The match had not been expected to take more than five days, but rain and the heavy roller repaired the pitch during the match and it was still in good condition for batting when the match was abandoned. The match became a test of endurance rather than cricketing skill. It did much to end the concept of timeless Tests, which were discontinued after World War Two.

A timeless Test is played under no limitation of time, which means the match is played until one side wins or the match is tied, with theoretically no possibility of a draw.

There were 99 timeless Tests between 1877 and 1939 and until World War Two all Tests in Australia were timeless.

The format was supposed to guarantee a result by taking weather delays and defensive play for a draw out of the equation. It was sometimes used for the final match of a series in order to ensure a winner.

However, better pitches and the lack of reasons for a batting side to declare meant huge totals became more commonplace. England had scored 903/7 at The Oval in a timeless Test in 1938. Several timeless matches had to be left unfinished as the tourists were at the mercy of shipping schedules.

The fifth Test between England and South Africa in 1939 lasted from 3 March to 14 March. Ten playing days took up 43 hours and 16 minutes on the field, 1,981 runs were scored and 12 new balls taken.

Afterwards, South Africa opener Pieter van der Bijl said: 'It has always puzzled me what the meaning of eternity is. Now I have a good idea.'

The opener top-scored in South Africa's first innings with a century. The home side racked up 530 after skipper Alan Melville had used a lucky coin to break Wally Hammond's run of correct calls at the toss. Dudley Nourse also scored a century in a first innings that lasted almost three days.

In reply, England could only manage 316, with wicketkeeper Les Ames top-scoring with 84. However, Melville declined to enforce the follow-on, instead aiming to pile on the runs and leave England a target he deemed impossible to reach.

In South Africa's second innings, Bruce Mitchell and van der Bijl combined for a first-wicket partnership of 191. Melville then added a century as South Africa were all out for 481, leaving England to chase 696.

Len Hutton scored a half-century before falling to Mitchell, which brought Bill Edrich to the crease. Edrich had endured a miserable tour, scoring only 21 runs in five innings to this point. He had got blind drunk on champagne the previous night, but the opener made light of his hangover to hit 219 runs.

There were further centuries for Paul Gibb and Hammond. By the time Hammond was out the match was almost at tea on the 12th day. England still needed 42 runs and had five wickets in hand.

However, their boat had departed Durban for Cape Town six days earlier and they needed to catch up with it by train. This meant it was the final day's play and the match had to be abandoned as a draw when the rain returned at tea and refused to relent for the rest of the day.

The Durban decider was the last of its kind after subjecting players and fans to a long and sometimes torturously slow match with a farcical ending. Hedley Verity had sent down 766 balls, a number only exceeded on one occasion since. Norman Gordon's tally of 738 remains the most delivered by a fast bowler in a Test.

Gordon said: 'I bowled 92 eight-ball overs in the timeless Test, which equals 120 six-ball overs, to get just one wicket. And I hope nobody has to go through something like that again.'

Many administrators were pushing for the end of timeless Tests as they caused problems with scheduling and pitches. Meanwhile, huge scores on over-prepared wickets with slow scoring rates were sucking the joy out of the game, as underlined at Kingsmead.

World War Two put the final nails in the coffin of timeless matches in England. The public had grown accustomed to shorter games played during the conflict and now wanted to see a more attractive style of cricket being played.

21

The Invincibles *(1948)*

THE 1948 Australian team that toured England has the rare distinction of being christened with its own nickname – The Invincibles. As the name suggests the side swept all before them, remaining undefeated against England, the counties and other teams while outscoring their opponents by wide margins.

In addition to featuring one of the greatest Test teams in cricket history the tour was also a farewell to the greatest batsman of all time, Don Bradman. Bradman made it known that he wanted to go through the tour unbeaten, a feat never before accomplished. English spectators turned out in their thousands to see the great man bat one final time.

Bradman captained the side, which featured a powerhouse batting line-up that included Lindsay Hassett, Bill Morris and the 19-year-old tyro Neil Harvey. Seven of the Australian batsmen passed 1,000 runs on the tour with an eighth, Sam Loxton, falling just 27 runs short due to a broken nose sustained against Yorkshire.

The 1948 team also included Keith Miller, widely regarded as Australia's best-ever all-rounder, and Ray Lindwall, one of the most fearsome fast bowlers the country has produced.

Bradman said: 'Knowing the personnel, I was confident that here at last was the great opportunity which I had longed for. A team of cricketers whose respect and loyalty were unquestioned, who would regard me in a fatherly sense and listen to my advice, follow my guidance and not question my handling of affairs.

'The result is a sense of freedom to give full reign to your own creative ability and personal judgement.'

On the 1948 tour, the Australians played 31 matches, winning 23, 15 by an innings, and drawing eight, often in matches where time was lost to the weather. Their batsmen averaged 50-plus per wicket throughout the tour compared to the 19.66 managed by the opposition batsmen. The Australian batters compiled 47 hundreds between them while their bowlers only conceded seven.

The Australians made 350 or more in 24 innings whereas, apart from the Tests, the highest total against them was Nottinghamshire's 299/8. The Australians failed to reach 200 only twice, but they dismissed opponents for less than that figure no fewer than 37 times and under 100 seven times.

The tour was a financial success too as spectators came out in large numbers to see Bradman and his all-powerful team play. Attendances created records in many parts of the country and the Australians received around £75,000 as their share of the profits, more than double the previous highest from an English tour.

Most importantly, the tourists retained the Ashes with a comprehensive 4-0 win over England while becoming the first side to complete a tour of the country unbeaten.

According to *Wisden*: 'In retaining the Ashes held by Australia since 1934, these Australians enjoyed almost uninterrupted success, while becoming the first side to go unbeaten through an English tour: certainly they achieved all that could be expected of a combination entitled to the description great. Yet they gave cause for reservation of such sweeping judgement as the Tests were by no means so one-sided as results suggested, and Yorkshire and Hampshire played themselves into positions arousing visions of the first Australian defeat by a county since Hampshire beat the 1912 team.

'Still, for the most part, victory followed victory so inevitably for the Australians that at times opponents took on an air of defeat almost before the match had been in progress more than an hour or two. Once or twice that impression extended even to the Tests.'

Although Bradman's powers were on the wane, as he passed his 40th birthday while on the tour, the great batsman still managed to score 11 centuries and amass 2,428 runs at an average of 89.92.

His highest score of the tour was 187 against Essex, when Australia compiled a world record of 721 runs in a day. In the Tests, he scored a memorable 173 in Australia's record-breaking win at Headingley.

In his autobiography, Bradman wrote: 'I was more sedate. I relied more on placing than on power and could not maintain for very long a period of solid aggression. On numerous occasions I threw my innings away rather than take the risk of breaking down.

'I did what I thought was more important at 40 – saw the tour through. I realised it was time to make way for a younger man.'

Despite this admission, Bradman began the tour with his traditional century at Worcester and started the Test series the same way with 138 at Trent Bridge. His century in the first Test came as Australia compiled a first-innings total of 509 in response to England's below-par 165. Although England recovered to score a respectable 441 in their second innings and force the visitors to bat again, Australia cruised to an eight-wicket victory.

The second Test at Lord's was even more one-sided with Lindwall taking eight wickets while the batsmen amassed totals of 350 and 460/7 declared to secure a huge win.

England threatened to bounce back in the third Test at Old Trafford, thanks largely to an unbeaten 145 from Denis Compton in the first innings. Alec Bedser then took 4-81 as the tourists were bowled out for 221. After the fourth day was lost to rain England set Australia a target of 317 but with further time lost to the elements, neither side came close to forcing a result.

In the fourth Test at Headingley, England scored 496 in their first innings with Cyril Washbrook hitting 143 and Australia replied with 458, thanks to a Harvey century. England then scored 365/8 before declaring on the last morning of the game, setting Australia a world record 404 runs to win in only 345 minutes on a heavily worn pitch.

However, Bradman's century, in partnership with Arthur Morris's 182, enabled the Australians to seal a stunning victory with 15 minutes of the match to spare.

In the final Test at The Oval, Bradman walked out to bat in Australia's first innings. He received a standing ovation from the crowd and three cheers from the opposition. His Test batting average stood at 101.39.

Facing the wrist-spin of Eric Hollies, Bradman pushed forward to the second ball that he faced, was deceived by a googly and was bowled between bat and pad for a duck. An England batting collapse resulted in an innings defeat, denying Bradman the opportunity to bat again and so his career average finished at 99.94; if he had scored just four runs in his last innings, it would have been a perfect 100.

The result at The Oval sealed a 4-0 series win and secured the Ashes for Australia. The Invincibles had earned their place in the history of the game with an unbeaten tour that comprised brilliant individual performances, crushing team victories, records and a fitting farewell to Test cricket's greatest batsman.

22

Len Hutton becomes England's first professional captain of the 20th century *(1952)*

UP UNTIL halfway through the last century England's captain in every home Test match had been an amateur. Three of England's first six captains had been professionals – James Lillywhite, Alfred Shaw and Arthur Shrewsbury – but they had led sides in Australia. Moreover, no professional had captained England since Shrewsbury in 1887 and none at all during the 20th century.

In 1952, Len Hutton, the pre-eminent English batsman of his era, became the first professional to captain England during the 20th century and the first to do so in a home Test.

As the 1950s began class distinctions still prevailed in English cricket. Traditionally, captains at both Test and county level were amateurs. Typically, the amateurs went to public school and Oxbridge and did not rely on cricket for their income. The sport was still run and administered by amateurs and they maintained that professionals would not make good captains.

This was due to the belief that professionals would be too concerned by their own contracts, or making decisions regarding fellow professionals' livelihoods, to make the necessary decisions on the field.

Speaking in 1925, at Yorkshire's annual general meeting the club's president Lord Hawke said: 'Pray God, no professional will ever captain England. I love and admire them all, but we have always had an amateur skipper and when the day comes when we shall have no more amateurs captaining England, it will be a thousand pities.'

In 1938, Wally Hammond had to switch from being a professional to a 'gentleman' to allow him to become England captain.

However, the situation often bordered on the absurd with counties frequently struggling to find amateurs to fulfil the captaincy. Professionals had to play under amateur captains who were often unable to claim a place in the team on merit. Some county captains were so poor that they did little more than stand on the field while the senior professionals made the decisions.

There were also 'shamateurs', players who were employed either by the county in an administrative role, or by a friendly business. Their duties would deliberately be light, allowing them to earn a living off the field while claiming amateur status on it.

When Freddie Brown resigned the England captaincy at the end of the 1951 season the assumption that his successor should be another amateur came under scrutiny. The following year, the England selectors – including Brown – judged that none of the serving amateur county captains possessed the required ability or experience to fill the role of England captain.

Yorkshire's Len Hutton was England's outstanding batsman of the era and the choice of many to take over; even so, the player himself harboured doubts about whether a professional captain would be accepted in some quarters. Despite these doubts the selectors appointed Hutton to captain England in the first Test of a four-match series against the 1952 Indian tourists. However, the Yorkshireman declined to turn amateur, as Hammond had done 14 years earlier.

Nevertheless, the decision had been widely expected and was met with general approval.

Wisden wrote: 'In breaking with tradition and choosing a professional as captain the Selection Committee made a vital decision in the interests of England, because it should mean that in future no man will be picked as leader unless he is worth a place in the side.'

Hutton began his captaincy with a win over India in front of his home crowd at Headingley. Although he failed with the bat and his tactics were cautious England won comfortably and Hutton was praised for his leadership. The result meant that he could continue as England captain.

England dominated India for the rest of the series, winning 3-0, with the final Test a rain-affected draw. Hutton scored 399 runs at an average of 79.80, including two centuries.

The following year Hutton was given the England captaincy on a match-by-match basis for a home Ashes series. A tight series saw the first four matches drawn while Hutton led from the front with 145 in the second Test at Lord's.

The final Test at The Oval gripped the nation as England aimed to reclaim the urn for the first time since 1934. Hutton's 82 ensured England had a slender first-innings lead. In reply, Australia collapsed to England's bowlers before Bill Edrich's half-century helped the home side to knock off the winning runs on the fourth day to seal a famous Ashes victory.

The following winter Hutton led England on a disappointing tour of the West Indies. The series was drawn with England coming back from 2-0 down to square the series and Hutton excelled with the bat, including a double century in the crucial final Test. However, the tour was overshadowed by issues including race, politics and umpiring decisions (see Moment 23).

Despite the problems faced on this tour and the fact that he missed large parts of the 1954 domestic season on medical advice, Hutton was chosen to lead the 1954/55 Ashes tour to Australia.

After suffering an innings defeat in the opening Test in Brisbane, the tourists bounced back to win three Tests in a row to retain the Ashes. Hutton's ability to see the potential of Frank Tyson's bowling with a shorter run-up was vital to the victory. Tyson took 26 wickets during the series as Hutton became only the second England captain after Percy Chapman to win successive Ashes series.

Health reasons forced Hutton to resign the England captaincy the following summer but his win-loss record of 11-4 remains among the best by an England captain. Apart from his batting skills, Hutton also showed himself to be an astute captain of the national team, despite never having led his county. His own batting performance was also consistent despite the demands of captaincy – he averaged over 52 in 23 Tests as captain.

Although the England captaincy would return to the amateurs for the next decade, Hutton had proved that a professional could excel in the role.

23

England make turbulent tour of West Indies *(1953/54)*

WHEN ENGLAND set out to tour the West Indies in late 1953 the series was billed as an unofficial world championship that would see the two best Test sides of the time face off.

The tour witnessed some great individual performances by some of the most famous names in cricket history. It also saw a great England comeback as they recovered from 2-0 down to draw the series. Yet, the tour is remembered for all the wrong reasons as it was beset with problems on and off the field.

England captain Len Hutton got the tour off to a bad start when he announced there would be no fraternising with the opposition and relations between the teams deteriorated from that point onwards. The West Indians were disappointed by the England team's reluctance to socialise as well as the defensive nature of the tourists' cricket.

Some of those who played in the series have argued it was more acrimonious than Bodyline.

On the field there was hostile bowling, batting collapses and a bowler no-balled for throwing. England were unhappy with the standard of the umpiring and the home crowds were not impressed either with trouble breaking out at two Tests.

Meanwhile, the West Indies' selection policies set the islands against each other and turned their captain, Jeff Stollmeyer, into a hate figure.

England's problems began before the team even departed with some critics questioning the choice of Hutton as captain. They argued that a professional captain was unsuitable to lead a tour.

The appointment of Leicestershire captain Charles Palmer, who was already selected as a player, as tour manager only served to undermine Hutton further. The England captain also found captaining some of the professionals in the party difficult, particularly wicketkeeper Godfrey Evans and fast bowler Fred Trueman.

The first Test set the tone for the troubled series with the wife and son of umpire Perry Burke attacked in the crowd after he gave the West Indies' John Holt out lbw on 94. And Tony Lock was no-balled for throwing, the first such call in a Test in the 20th century.

Holt's 94 helped the West Indies to compile 417 in their first innings at Sabina Park in Kingston, Jamaica. England could only muster 170 in reply and Stollmeyer was booed by the crowd for not enforcing the follow-on.

Everton Weekes scored 90 as the home side set the tourists a target of 457 to win. England collapsed from 277/2 to 316 all out as the West Indies went 1-0 up with a 140-run victory.

The second Test followed a similar pattern. The home side batted first, with Clyde Walcott scoring a magnificent 220, out of a first-innings total of 383. England scored 181 in reply, but Stollmeyer once again declined to enforce the follow-on.

Holt completed a century in the second innings as the West Indies added 292/2 leaving England with a target of 495 to win. The tourists reached 258/3 before another collapse left them all out for 313.

England won the third Test, which was played in a febrile atmosphere in Georgetown, Guyana. The country's constitution was suspended at the time, while its elected nationalist leader, Cheddi Jagan, had returned home for the first time since British troops had removed him from office the previous year.

On the field Hutton scored 169 after winning the toss and electing to bat. In reply to England's 435 the West Indies were all out for 251. Weekes top-scored with 90 but missiles were thrown on to the outfield when Cliff McWatt was run out on 54. However, Hutton kept his team and the umpires on the field, possibly defusing a dangerous situation. Following on, West Indies scored 256 and England duly knocked off the 73 runs required for victory for the loss of three wickets.

The fourth Test in Trinidad was played on a flat pitch and it took five days to complete the two first innings. West Indies' 681/8 declared was the highest score by a West Indies cricket team at the time. Weekes made 206, Frank Worrell 167 and Walcott 124. England made 537 in reply, with centuries from Peter May and Denis Compton and 92 from Tom Graveney. The game ended in a draw.

The teams returned to Jamaica for the fifth and final Test with England requiring victory to level the series. The match saw the debut of a 17-year-old Garry Sobers.

Although the West Indies got first use of what appeared to be a perfect pitch for batting, they were bowled out for 139 as Bailey took 7-34, his best Test return. England's reply of 414 was based on a brilliant double century for Hutton.

The innings ended amid yet another controversy when local officials and journalists accused Hutton of snubbing the congratulations of Jamaica's Chief Minister Alexander Bustamante during a tea interval. Hutton apologised, claiming not to have noticed Bustamante speaking to him, but was dismissed immediately after play resumed.

Although Walcott made his third century of the series the West Indies could only set England a target of 72 to level the series. Although Graveney was out for a duck in the first over, Willie Watson and May saw the target reached with ease to make it 2–2.

Wisden's review of the series was critical of almost all of those involved. It recommended that the West Indies draw up a panel of umpires from all the islands rather than using local umpires in each match.

But it also had harsh words for England players whose dissent was made public and also for the excessive caution of the England team in the second Test. The experiment of using a player-manager on a controversial tour, *Wisden* said, was also 'not to be commended'.

The tour not only prompted changes to cricket and touring for both teams but was also one of the times when sport and politics clashed as the desire for independence grew across the Caribbean.

24

Seminal series starts with first tied Test *(1960)*

The Gabba, Brisbane, 9–14 December 1960

First Test

West Indies	Australia
453	505
Sobers 132	O'Neill 181
Davidson 5-135	Hall 4-140
284	232
Worrell 65	Davidson 80
Davidson 6-87	Hall 5-63

Match tied

THE OPENING match of the 1960/61 series between Australia and the West Indies came to a nail-biting climax before giving Test cricket its first ever tie – the rarest result in the sport. The match teed up a thrilling series that also saw the final two Tests go down to the wire.

Although the series was the first time the Australian Broadcasting Corporation had covered all five Test matches of a tour, it did not prevent record crowds flocking to the grounds to watch the action live.

The West Indies, who were being captained by their first full-time black captain Frank Worrell, may have lost the series 2-1 but gained many friends and admirers and were given a heroes' send-off by the Melbourne public.

Worrell and his opposing captain, Richie Benaud, both received many plaudits for encouraging their teams to play attacking cricket and the spirit in which the series was played.

The series was in marked contrast to the cricket played in the preceding decade, which had often been slow, dull and attritional. Slow scoring rates, chucking and beamers were rife on the pitch during the 1950s while there had been riots at Tests in the West Indies and India.

It was the tie in Brisbane that provided the spark, setting up a series that offered Test cricket a glimpse of a brighter future.

The match began with a brilliant Garry Sobers century, the all-rounder scoring 132 in only 174 minutes. Sobers' hundred rescued the West Indies from a poor start – they were 65/3 after Alan Davidson removed the top order – to help them finish the first day on 359/7.

On the next morning, Gerry Alexander took his overnight score of 21 to 60 while Wes Hall, who was batting at ten, scored a half-century as the West Indies were all out for 453.

Both Australian openers passed 50 in the home side's reply with Bob Simpson falling just short of his hundred shortly before the close of play.

On the third day, Australia took a first-innings lead of 52, thanks mainly to Norm O'Neill's 181. The lead could have been larger but the tail collapsed from 406/5 to 505 all out.

The West Indies closed day four on 259/9 having slipped from 210/4 with Rohan Kanhai and Worrell passing 50 but no batsman able to post the large score that could put the match beyond Australia's reach.

However, the following morning the last West Indies pair added 25 vital runs and used up valuable time from that available for the Australian run chase. The home side were set a target of 233 to win from 69 eight-ball overs.

A fired-up Hall then proceeded to tear through the Australian top order, taking four wickets as the home side were reduced to 92/6. The match then swung back in Australia's favour thanks to a stand of 118 put on by Davidson and Benaud.

With victory in sight Benaud called for a sharp single, but Joe Solomon hit the stumps from midwicket to dismiss Davidson for 80.

The new batsman, Wally Grout, took a single from the last ball of the over. This left Australia needing six runs from the final over of the day, which was to be bowled by Hall, with three wickets in hand.

Benaud called Grout through for a leg bye on the first ball, but was caught behind hooking the next ball. Two scrambled runs left Grout and Ian Meckiff needing three from three, but Meckiff found Conrad Hunte at midwicket and his brilliant return created the first of two sensational run-outs.

Australia were now poised on 232/9 with the teams tied. One run was needed off two balls, with one wicket remaining. Lindsay Kline nudged the ball to square leg and tried to steal the single that would win the game but Solomon threw down the stumps to give Test cricket its first ever tied match.

Davidson, who had scored 124 runs and taken 11 wickets in the match, said: 'There were so many great moments in the Test match. You can always say this bloke played a great innings, or someone bowled well, but there were so many wonderful moments.

'Joe Solomon ran me out in the second-last over – he threw the wicket down. And then he turns around and throws the wicket down to tie the match. In the circumstances and the pressure there would have been there for the fielding side, that was amazing.

'There was confusion everywhere. I don't think anybody knew. There were broadcasters who were mixed up. Rohan Kanhai was running around with his arms above his head, saying, "We are the champions, we are the champions!" I think he thought that they'd won. It was the most amazing situation.'

The second and third Tests were one-sided affairs. Australia won by seven wickets in Melbourne and the West Indies hit back with a 222-run victory in Sydney thanks to another Sobers century.

The series was tied at 1-1 as the teams moved on to Adelaide, where they served up another thriller.

A high-scoring match saw Kanhai hitting centuries in both West Indies innings. The tourists scored 393 in their first innings with Worrell contributing 71 and Benaud taking 5-96.

The Australian reply was anchored by Simpson's 85 while a useful 35 from Des Hoare, batting at number ten in his only Test match, helped them to 366, a deficit of just 27.

In addition to Kanhai's second hundred of the match, Worrell, Alexander and Hunte all passed 50 as the West Indies made 432/6 before declaring and leaving Australia a mammoth 461 to win.

Australia made a terrible start to their innings and ended day four on 32/3, with Hall taking the wickets of Simpson and Les Favell after McDonald had been run out.

The home side lost a steady stream of wickets on the final day and appeared to be on the verge of defeat at 207/9. Despite useful knocks from O'Neill, Peter Burge and Ken Mackay the victory target looked out of reach and survival impossible.

In one of the great rearguard actions, Mackay and last man Lindsay Kline proceeded to play out the remaining time while the West Indies desperately searched for the vital last wicket. Mackay's 62 not out occupied 223 balls, and Kline's 15, his highest-ever Test score, was made from 109.

The teams returned to Melbourne for the deciding Test with the West Indies batting first again and scoring 292. The second day was a Saturday, and a then world record crowd of 90,800 turned up at the Melbourne Cricket Ground to watch. Australia reached 236/3 by the end of the day's play after Simpson and McDonald put on 146 for the first wicket.

The home side finished on 356, a lead of 64, with Sobers and spinner Lance Gibbs sharing nine wickets between them. In response, the West Indies posted 321 as Alexander top-scored with 73. Hunte was the only other batsman to pass 50 as a victory target of 258 was set.

Simpson's 92 gave Australia a great start but wickets fell steadily through the last day.

O'Neill, Neil Harvey and Davidson were all dismissed by Worrell and when Peter Burge was seventh out to Valentine for 53, Australia still needed another eight runs to win.

Grout enjoyed a moment of luck when the umpires ruled that he was not out despite a bail falling to the floor but was dismissed by Valentine to make the score 256/8. Mackay, who scored 3 from 51 balls, and Johnny Martin managed to hang on and see Australia over the line for a two-wicket win that clinched the series.

It was heartbreak for the tourists, who could have quite easily won the series 3-1 if a couple of key moments had gone their way.

There was some compensation as the team were paraded through Melbourne in open-top cars and cheered by enormous crowds, a send-off normally reserved for royalty and national heroes.

Worrell said: 'Never before had we experienced the pleasure of playing cricket in an environment in which the spectators regarded the quality of cricket as all-important whilst they seemed completely disinterested in the result of the game.

'The statement which was quite frequently made and which brought a lump to my throat and tears to my eyes: "Come back soon."'

25

The Midlands Knockout Cup *(1962)*

IN 1962, an experimental tournament called the Midlands Knockout Cup was played over two Wednesdays between four English counties in front of modest crowds.

The competition was a qualified success but did enough to prove that limited-overs cricket at first-class level had real potential. It was from the humble beginnings of the Midlands tournament that limited-overs cricket has flourished with knockout cups, leagues, television deals, sponsorship, internationals matches and World Cups all following.

The idea for one-day cricket had begun in the Indian state of Kerala in 1951 with the 50-over All India Pooja Cricket Tournament. Although this competition continues to this day it does not have List A status.

Ten years later the English and Welsh cricket authorities were concerned about attendances at County Championship matches and looking for ideas.

The idea of a limited-overs knockout competition was discussed by the advisory body governing English cricket. Leicestershire secretary Mike Turner attended that meeting at The Oval, which ended with an agreement in principle to trial a limited-overs tournament in 1963.

Turner spotted an opportunity to stage a trial run a year earlier and came up with the idea for the Midlands Knockout Cup.

Turner said: 'I saw some gaps in the fixture list and phoned around. My opposite numbers jumped at the chance. By the early 60s we had reached the end of cricket's post-war boom. The crowds had declined and there was a need to make the game viable. These were parlous times and there were arguments about which direction the game should take.'

The first two Wednesdays of that season showed space for Leicestershire, Nottinghamshire, Derbyshire and Northamptonshire to play in the experiment. The knockout tournament was 65 overs per side with bowlers restricted to a maximum of 15 overs each.

The two semi-finals were played on Wednesday, 2 May 1962, with Northants beating Notts at Trent Bridge by 31 runs and Leicestershire knocking out Derbyshire at Grace Road by seven runs. A week later Northants triumphed in the final by five wickets.

Although crowds were low – only 1,000 turned up to watch the final at Grace Road – the tournament did enough to prove the concept worked. Crucially, it had attracted commercial television coverage, which in turn meant sponsorship was a possibility. Media reports had been positive as the cricket had been exciting and even the low crowds could be excused as the weather had been colder than usual for May.

The following summer, the Gillette Cup, the world's first domestic knockout tournament for first-class sides, started and was an immediate success. Crowds flocked to the matches and the Lord's final became an established full-house finale to the English cricket season. It was also the first sponsored event of its kind thanks to the support of US razor company Gillette.

Fittingly, Leicestershire took part in the new tournament's opening match against Lancashire at Old Trafford, which lasted two days due to rain. The home side's Peter Marner scored the Gillette Cup's first century as Lancashire set an imposing target of 304. Marner then combined with Brian Statham, who took the competitions first 'five for', to bowl out Leicestershire and set up victory by 101 runs, despite a century from the visitors' skipper Maurice Hallam.

The first Lord's final saw Ted Dexter's Sussex claim the inaugural trophy thanks to the efforts of Man of the Match Norman Gifford. The match was played in poor batting conditions with Sussex bowled out for just 168. However, Gifford's 4-33 helped Sussex bowl out Worcestershire for 154 to secure a 14-run victory.

The second season of the competition saw the introduction of five minor counties and the possibility of FA Cup-style giant-killings. The most famous of these was Durham's victory over Yorkshire in 1973.

For almost 30 years, the Gillette Cup (which became the NatWest Trophy in 1981) provided domestic midweek entertainment through the summer as well as the traditional end-of-season climax on the first Saturday in September. Lancashire were the tournament's most successful side with seven wins, including three in a row from 1970 to 1972.

More importantly, the success of the Gillette Cup opened up possibilities for other one-day competitions around the globe. In England, the John Player Sunday League had been launched by the end of the decade. And the first one-day international was played in 1971 as England took on Australia in Melbourne after the New Year Test had been washed out (see Moment 28).

Four years later the men's Cricket World Cup was launched with the West Indies beating Australia in the final at Lord's to become the first ever champions. Limited-overs cricket was here to stay. Many formats have followed with the overs being reduced from 65 a side to 60, 50 or 40 before the advent of Twenty20 cricket. Knockout competitions, franchise cricket, leagues and global tournaments have all followed a concept proven by four county sides in the English Midlands in 1962.

26

The County Championship opens the door to overseas stars *(1968)*

IN 1968, the County Championship began welcoming the world's greatest players after relaxing the rules on residential qualification. Following the rule change, county clubs were permitted to sign one overseas player who could appear for them that summer.

The ruling opened the door for some of the best talents in the world game to grace county grounds. The first summer alone saw Garry Sobers, Mike Procter, Barry Richards, Greg Chappell, Asif Iqbal and Farokh Engineer amongst those who signed up.

There had long been a few foreign nationals playing in the county game despite residential rules dating back to 1873. Those rules had been introduced following rows about the importing of 'colonial cricketers'. This was due to the tension between those who thought a county side should represent its area and those that wanted to focus on winning the title.

Following the Second World War, the rise of immigration from the Commonwealth led to some overseas players giving up playing for their countries of birth and settling in England.

However, prior to 1968 most overseas players in England played league cricket, which had less stringent residency rules and paid as well as county cricket. Those foreign stars helped attract good crowds to league cricket, inevitably drawing envious glances from the county clubs.

Nottinghamshire wanted Sobers to play for them and proposed a change in the rules, which was agreed by the Test and County Cricket Board.

Sobers had already played for Radcliffe in the Central Lancashire League as well as South Australia, where his performances had nearly doubled gate receipts. The chance to sign the West Indies all-rounder precipitated a bidding war, with Lancashire and Gloucestershire losing out to Nottinghamshire's offer of a salary of up to £7,000, along with a flat to live in and a car to drive.

Sobers repaid Nottinghamshire by providing one of the sport's most famous moments. On 31 August 1968 at Swansea, he hit Glamorgan's Malcolm Nash for six sixes in an over. It was a seminal moment as county cricket entered a new age and one that was destined to be replayed countless times on television screens over the following years.

Engineer joined Lancashire, who had not won a trophy for 18 years, where he was joined by West Indies great Clive Lloyd a year later, when the rules were relaxed further to allow two overseas players per county. The Indian wicketkeeper-batsman stayed at Old Trafford until 1976, by which time Lancashire had won four Gillette Cups and the John Player Sunday League.

Procter was signed by Gloucestershire where he would stay for 14 seasons, captaining them for five, scoring over 14,000 runs and taking more than 800 wickets. The South African also helped Gloucestershire win their first piece of silverware – the 1973 Gillette Cup – scoring a vital 94 against Sussex in the final.

Barry Richards went to Hampshire, Chappell was signed by Somerset while Iqbal headed for Canterbury and Kent.

These players were the first wave of many over the next few decades that saw county cricket graced by a host of international greats including Imran Khan, Shane Warne, Wasim Akram, Viv Richards, Richard Hadlee, Muttiah Muralitharan, Joel Garner, Glenn McGrath, Brian Lara, Allan Donald and many more.

It took until 1992 for Yorkshire to finally become the last county to sign an overseas player – or even one born outside the county. The honour went to a 19-year-old Sachin Tendulkar, who had made his India debut at 16 and scored his maiden Test century at Old Trafford two years earlier (see Moment 37). Tendulkar played 16 first-class matches for the county and scored 1,070 runs at an average of 46.52.

The 'Little Master' did suffer disappointment on his Yorkshire debut though, despite scoring 86 against a Hampshire attack boasting Malcolm Marshall. 'I always make a hundred in my first match,' commented Tendulkar afterwards.

The impact of overseas stars on county cricket during the 1970s and 1980s was exacerbated by two forces.

Firstly, the abundance of talent available to the West Indies during this era. This meant that not only the Test greats including Lloyd, Viv Richards, Garner, Andy Roberts, Alvin Kallicharran, Gordon Greenidge, Rohan Kanhai, Michael Holding and Desmond Haynes starred for counties. In addition, formidable bowlers like Wayne Daniels and Sylvester Clarke were fixtures in the Championship, despite being underused in international cricket.

Clarke, who took almost a thousand first-class wickets at less than 20 but played only 11 Tests and Daniel, who took 867 wickets at 22.47 yet made just ten Test appearances, were county cricket superstars.

Meanwhile, South Africa's apartheid-era exclusion from international cricket meant that many of the country's finest cricketers beat a path to the counties in order to find an appropriate stage for their talents.

Procter and Barry Richards were joined by a host of their countrymen. Eddie Barlow and Peter Kirsten played for Derbyshire, Clive Rice went to Nottinghamshire, Lee Irvine and Kenny McEwan played for Essex, Garth le Roux was at Sussex, Jimmy Cook at Somerset and Donald at Warwickshire.

Procter and Engineer were not the only members of the foreign legion to help their counties to success. In 1973, the batting of Barry Richards and Greenidge helped fire Hampshire to their second County Championship title. At Somerset, Garner and Viv Richards inspired Somerset to the Gillette Cup and John Player League in 1979, the B&H Cup in 1981 and 1982, and the NatWest Trophy in 1983 – easily the most successful spell in their history. Hadlee and Rice inspired Nottinghamshire to the Championship in 1981 – their first in 52 years – and again in 1987, when they also won the NatWest Trophy.

However, these successes came at a price with some claiming that the benefits overseas players brought to county cricket were outweighed by a perceived cost to the England team, which was undergoing mixed fortunes. Many of the overseas stars cut their teeth in county cricket before maturing into Test cricketers. Some thought this was not only blocking the progress of England's youngsters but also gave the overseas stars invaluable experience of English conditions.

In 1982, a new rule allowing the counties to field just one overseas player in Championship matches was introduced. In 1991, that was tightened to one per squad.

Further changes came from an unexpected source in 2003 following a decision in the European Court of Justice concerning Slovakian handball goalkeeper Maros Kolpak.

Following this, citizens of any country with a free trade agreement with the EU were eligible to work within it, and that included Jamaicans, Zimbabweans and South Africans. This led to another influx of foreign players into county cricket.

The Kolpak change also coincided with a reduction in the number of overseas cricketers playing for one county for many seasons. Instead, overseas players began to dip in and out of county cricket, sometimes fitting in just a few games between international commitments and switching counties as necessary. In 2023, this saw India's Cheteshwar Pujara and Australia's Steve Smith batting together for Sussex before facing each other in the World Test Championship Final weeks later.

However, all this was made possible by the relaxation of the qualification laws in 1968, a decision that spawned a golden era for county cricket.

27

The D'Oliveira Affair *(1968)*

THE D'OLIVEIRA Affair transcended cricket as a furore over one player's selection for an England tour had consequences going beyond the sport and impacting on both international politics and the history of South Africa.

The Affair helped spark the sporting boycott of South Africa, contributing to the end of the racist apartheid system and helping create the modern Rainbow Nation.

When Marylebone Cricket Club (MCC) called off the tour of South Africa scheduled for the winter of 1968/69 it signalled the start of South Africa's sporting isolation. The cancellation happened because the South African government would not accept the presence of Basil D'Oliveira, a so-called 'coloured' cricketer from Cape Town, in the England tour party.

D'Oliveira had started the summer of 1968 with an unbeaten 87 in the second innings of the first Ashes Test against Australia. However, that match ended in a heavy 159-run defeat for England and D'Oliveira was one of those who paid the price as he was dropped for the following three Tests.

However, he was recalled to the England side for the final Test of the series because of an illness to Roger Prideaux. D'Oliveira responded in superb style with a brilliant innings of 158 to help England square the Ashes series.

More significantly, it appeared that this innings had done enough to earn D'Oliveira a place on that winter's England tour of South Africa.

The tour of his native South Africa had been D'Oliveira's ambition since he made his debut for his adopted country two years earlier.

The potential for the cricketer to return home with England hadn't gone unnoticed in South Africa either, where cricket officials and politicians knew his inclusion would lead to the tour being cancelled. So, pressure was exerted on the MCC hierarchy leading to the decision not to pick him and D'Oliveira was surprisingly omitted from the squad.

He said: 'I kept waiting to hear my name in the list of players but it wasn't there. I was dumbstruck.

'I don't know how long I stood there but the first thing I recall was Tom Graveney swearing bitterly and saying: "I never thought they'd do that to you, Bas." Tom saw the state I was in and he took me into the physio's room where I broke down and sobbed like a baby.

'Doug Insole [chairman of the England selectors] said I wasn't one of the 16 best players in England at that time, so I wasn't selected on purely cricketing grounds. I left it to the national press to state my case.'

The press responded by vigorously questioning the batsman's omission while a group of MCC members, led by the Reverend David Sheppard, a former Test batsman, accused the club of placating the South African authorities in order to save the tour. This group put down a motion of censure over MCC's handling of the matter while the club received over 1,000 letters of protest.

However, there was a twist in the tale when Warwickshire bowler Tom Cartwright was forced to withdraw from the England touring party with injury. Despite the fact that

D'Oliveira was predominantly a batsman he was drafted into the squad to replace Cartwright.

D'Oliveira said: 'I didn't care about the fact that the selectors were now choosing me as an all-rounder when a fortnight earlier they'd justified their decision to exclude me by saying that I was being judged purely as a batsman. That didn't matter anymore – the goal was again in sight and the well-wishers were again slapping me on the back.'

The response from South African Prime Minister John Vorster was swift as he claimed that the England team was now representative of the anti-apartheid movement.

He said: 'We are not prepared to accept a team thrust upon us ... it is the team of political opponents of South Africa. It is a team of people who don't care about sports relations at all.'

This left MCC with little option but to cancel the tour and England would not play South Africa again until the early 1990s. That followed the exclusion of the Proteas from Test cricket for 22 years as the country suffered a sporting boycott until the abolition of apartheid.

Born and raised on the outskirts of Cape Town, D'Oliveira, who was often nicknamed Dolly, was a talented sportsman. He played cricket for Western Province, led a non-white South African representative side on a 1958 tour of Kenya and also played football for a national non-white team.

Although best known for his batting exploits, he was also a shrewd swing bowler with a handy knack for breaking partnerships. Despite generally being regarded as the finest non-white South African player of his generation, D'Oliveira was unable to play Test cricket due to the apartheid regime.

It was a letter to the English cricket commentator John Arlott in 1958 that led, two years later, to a move to England

and a contract with Middleton, a Central Lancashire League club. He would eventually graduate to play county cricket for Worcestershire. In 1965, his first full county season, he finished fifth in the national batting averages, behind four Test players. A year later he made his England debut at Lord's against the West Indies.

D'Oliveira went on to play 44 Tests for England, scoring 2,484 runs at an average of 40, and picking up 47 wickets. He played for Worcestershire until 1980 before taking over as the county's coach for a decade. In all first-class matches he scored 19,490 runs at 40.26 and took 551 wickets at 27.45.

Speaking after D'Oliveira's death in 2011, Peter Hain, the former Labour MP and anti-apartheid campaigner said: 'He was somebody who just carried himself in a very dignified way, despite all the pressures whirling around him. Somebody who became much loved in the English cricket world as a result and yet somebody who, in his own quiet, modest and unassuming way, became the symbol of what was wrong with apartheid South Africa.'

The D'Oliveira Affair was a watershed moment in the sporting boycott of apartheid South Africa. It also had a far-reaching impact in turning international opinion against the apartheid regime in South Africa. Although it took many years, the Affair helped put South Africa on the road to major changes in its sport, society and politics.

28

Abandoned Test leads
to the first ODI *(1971)*

Melbourne Cricket Ground, Melbourne, 5 January 1971

One-Day International

England	Australia
190	191/5
Edrich 82	I. Chappell 60
Mallett 3-34	Illingworth 3-50

Australia won by five wickets

AN ASHES washout in Melbourne led to the first-ever one-day international (ODI). The match between England and Australia was arranged in a hurry after a Test had been abandoned due to three days of incessant rain.

It may have been an unofficial match with an Australian XI taking on an England XI but it was a success, proving the limited-overs concept had potential at the international level. The first men's World Cup was played four years afterwards and later in the decade World Series Cricket would further increase the popularity of ODI cricket.

The match came about during the 1970/71 Ashes series in Australia. Following two slow, attritional draws in the opening two Tests of the series the teams headed to Melbourne for the third instalment. England captain Ray Illingworth won the toss and decided to field.

However, the weather intervened with rain starting to fall before play could start, and continuing for three days, until the match was abandoned without a ball being bowled.

The decision was controversial, with the Melbourne Cricket Ground's (MCG) ground staff desperately trying to dry the pitch out and claiming that the wicket was playable and bowlers' run-ups safe.

Meanwhile, the Australian cricket authorities were faced with a significant financial loss. They had been encouraging spectators to come to the MCG each day, promising that play would start as soon as the rain stopped. On the third day alone 8,000 hardy souls arrived at the ground only to be denied any cricket by the weather.

The prospect of the financial loss combined with the public's obvious appetite for cricket spurred the cricket authorities into action. The Australian board and Marylebone Cricket Club (MCC) agreed to schedule a seventh Test match to be played in Sydney, while improved weather conditions meant play was possible on what would have been the fifth day of the Test.

The authorities agreed on an ODI to consist of 40 eight-ball overs with one innings per side. No bowler would be allowed to bowl more than a fifth of the total number of overs per side. The Australian board even invited Sir Donald Bradman, who delivered a pre-match speech to both teams.

The cigarette firm Rothmans agreed to pay AUS$5,000 to sponsor the match. The winning team would earn AUS$2,400, the losers AUS$400 and the Man of the Match AUS$200. Despite the rain over the previous week just over 46,000 spectators paid almost AUS$34,000 to attend the game.

Australia's captain Bill Lawry won the toss and put England in to bat, which was the usual tactic in limited-overs cricket at the time.

England's openers Geoffrey Boycott and John Edrich were both noted for their cautious, defensive style of play. However, the pair took to the new format with relish, unfurling previously unseen attacking strokes and running hard between the wickets. In response the Australian fielders threw themselves into the occasion with a new-found athleticism as they looked to reduce runs and cut off boundaries.

Australian fast bowler Alan Thomson took the first ever ODI wicket when he had Boycott caught for 8 by Lawry. However, it was the spin bowlers, usually regarded as a target in limited-overs matches, who did most of the damage. Ashley Mallett took 3-34 with his off spin while Keith Stackpole's part-time leg spin accounted for another three England wickets.

Edrich made 82 runs off 119 balls while wickets tumbled around him. No other England batsman made 25 and the Middlesex player was instrumental in England making a total of 190.

Australia reached the victory target of 191 with ease, thanks largely to vice-captain Ian Chappell and Doug Walters. It was Stackpole who set the tone for the Australian innings though, hitting John Snow's second over for 12 runs.

Chappell started slowly before accelerating with boundaries from Illingworth's bowling and 26 taken from two Basil D'Oliveira overs. Meanwhile, Walters made hay with 41 off 51 balls, including six fours as he added 66 with Chappell for the third wicket.

Illingworth was the best of the England bowlers but his 3-50 could not prevent Australia winning comfortably by five wickets. Despite finishing on the losing side Edrich was named Man of the Match by umpire Charlie Elliott, who said that 'without John's 82 there'd have been no match'.

Although the game had been one-sided it was deemed a success with the large crowd exceeding expectations. The media generally welcomed the new format and predicted it would bring excitement to the sport – although *Wisden* refused to publish a match report. Some commentators noted that the limited-overs format involved more tactical ploys and generally sharper fielding and running between the wickets.

This success and media attention was noted by administrators who could see the potential in the format. There were soon suggestions that every international tour should consist of two separate series for Tests and ODIs, a template that was followed throughout the cricketing world not long afterwards.

Even more crucially, the first men's World Cup followed in 1975 (see Moment 30) and proved a success leading to further editions every four years. That tournament has continued to grow over the years and despite the advent of Twenty20 cricket it remains one of the biggest and most sought-after prizes in cricket.

29

The first Cricket World Cup *(1973)*

THE FIRST ever global cricket tournament staged was the 1973 Women's Cricket World Cup, which took place fully two years earlier than the inaugural men's version.

The 60-over tournament was held in England between 20 June and 28 July 1973 and featured seven teams. England, Australia, New Zealand, Jamaica and Trinidad & Tobago were joined by an International XI and a Young England side in a round robin league with the top team becoming champions. The concluding match of the tournament brought together England and Australia who were the top two in the table, so it became a de facto final with the hosts triumphing at Edgbaston.

The tournament had been in the pipeline for two years with businessman Sir Jack Hayward promoting it and contributing £40,000 towards its costs.

There were four Test-playing nations in women's international cricket. However, South Africa were sporting pariahs due to apartheid and unable to participate. This left England, Australia and New Zealand in need of further opposition to make the tournament viable.

Hayward had previously organised tours of the West Indies by England women, so it was from this region that the other two competing nations were drawn with the inclusion of both Trinidad & Tobago and Jamaica.

The playing numbers were boosted further by the Young England and International XI teams. Initially, five South Africans were invited to play for the International XI as a means of compensation for the team not being invited, but those invitations were later withdrawn.

England captain Rachael Heyhoe Flint said: 'The inaugural tournament created huge public awareness of the very existence of women's cricket. That was a great bonus because even though the first recorded writings about women's cricket were in 1745, the general public in the UK were still very ignorant about us.'

The tournament got off to a disappointing start on 20 June when the opening match was abandoned without a ball being bowled due to rain.

Three days later the World Cup began in earnest as Australia cruised to a seven-wicket victory over Young England while England thrashed the International XI. England's Lynne Thomas scored the tournament's first century in the 135-run victory at Hove and her score of 134 proved to be the highest of the tournament.

The best bowling figures of the competition were recorded by New Zealand's Glenys Page, who took 6-24 in her side's 136-run victory over Trinidad & Tobago at Clarence Park in St Albans.

Going into the final match Australia led the table by a single point as they had won four matches. Crucially their match against the International XI at St Helen's in Swansea had been abandoned after less than five overs due to rain. England had also won four matches, but had lost to New Zealand.

It was England who triumphed in the final match of the tournament at Edgbaston, thanks to Enid Bakewell's century and 64 from Heyhoe Flint. Those knocks helped England to a formidable total of 279 in their 60 overs. Australia were restricted by tight England bowling and fell well short of the target, scoring 187/9.

That meant England topped the final table with 20 points from their six matches while Australia were runners-up, posting 17 points.

The cup was presented by Princess Anne and the winning England team were hosted at a reception at 10 Downing Street by Prime Minister Edward Heath.

Heyhoe Flint said: 'I remember the final more than any other game of course – we won it. I was so nervous because of the media and royal attention that I took four overs to get off the mark. But I got a half-century and led England to the title. Princess Anne handed the trophy to us.'

Bakewell was the leading run-scorer in the competition with 264 runs while Rosalind Heggs, of Young England, was the leading wicket-taker with 12.

The next Women's World Cup was held five years later in 1978 and although the tournament was sporadic in its early years, since 2005 it has settled into being staged at regular four-year intervals.

The 12 Women's World Cups played to date have been held in five countries, with India and England each having hosted the event three times.

Australia are the most successful team, having won seven titles and failed to make the final on only three occasions. England are the next most successful team with four titles while New Zealand have claimed one. India and the West Indies are the only other sides to reach a final although both had to settle for the runners-up spot.

Australia are the current champions after beating England to clinch the 2022 edition of the tournament thanks to Alyssa Healey's monumental 170, which set up a 71-run win.

The 2022 World Cup underlined how the tournament now attracts big crowds and worldwide television coverage. It showed how far the game has come since the humble beginnings of the pioneering 1973 edition in England.

30

The West Indies conquer the world
(1975)

THE FIRST men's World Cup took place in 1975 and saw the West Indies conquer the world of cricket after Clive Lloyd's men saw off Australia in a thrilling final at Lord's.

The inaugural global men's tournament took place in England with eight teams playing 60-overs-a-side matches in traditional white clothing and with red balls. There were no floodlights so all the matches were played in daylight hours.

Eight teams were invited to compete at the World Cup. Six of those nations were the full members of the International Cricket Council (ICC): England, Australia, West Indies, New Zealand, India and Pakistan.

South Africa were isolated due to apartheid and would not compete in a World Cup until 1992. Instead Africa was represented by East Africa, an amalgamation of amateur club cricketers from Kenya, Uganda, Tanzania and Zambia. The final competitor was Sri Lanka, the strongest associate nation of the era.

England hosted the tournament with its six traditional Test match grounds providing the venues. Even the English weather co-operated with the organisers and not an over was lost to rain as June 1975 provided perfect sunshine.

One-day internationals (ODIs) were still in their infancy; it was a mere four years since England and Australia had played the first one. However, domestic limited-overs competitions were underway in England and those who had played in them had an advantage. This included the entire West Indies team, who were installed as the bookmakers' favourites to win the tournament.

Many teams and spectators still looked upon these matches as effectively one-day Test cricket. Never was this more apparent than in England and India's opening match in Group A at Lord's on 7 June. England racked up 334 in their 60 overs, the highest score in an ODI at the time. Dennis Amiss top-scored for England with 137 from 147 balls helped by Keith Fletcher and Chris Old, who each recorded a half-century.

In response, India batted cautiously throughout their 60 overs, finishing on 123/3. Gundappa Viswanath top-scored with 37 while opener Sunil Gavaskar carried his bat through the innings for 36. The Indian team manager, Gulabrai Ramchand, later commented that he thought Gavaskar was using the match as batting practice.

Three other matches took place on the opening day. The other match in Group A saw New Zealand cruise to an easy 180-run win over East Africa. Kiwi opener Glenn Turner carried his bat for an unbeaten 171, and would finish the tournament as top run-scorer with 333.

In Group B, Australia opened their campaign with a win against Pakistan at Headingley with a 73-run victory. Australia set Pakistan a target of 278 with Ross Edwards scoring 80 and the tail wagging to add 94 runs in the final 13 overs. In reply, Pakistan collapsed from 181/4 to 205 all out as Dennis Lillee took five wickets.

The other match in the group saw West Indies cruise to an easy nine-wicket victory over Sri Lanka, who became the first team to score under 100 runs in an ODI.

Many observers rated the meeting between Pakistan and the West Indies in the second round of games as the match of the tournament. Pakistan desperately needed a win to have any chance of progressing to the semi-finals after their opening loss.

However, they were without Asif Iqbal, who needed an operation, and Imran Khan, who was sitting exams at Oxford University. Instead, a young Javed Miandad made his debut and contributed a useful 24 as Pakistan reached 266/7. Majid Khan top-scored with 60.

Victory appeared to be in Pakistan's grasp as the West Indies struggled to 166/8. However, wicketkeeper Deryck Murray put on 37 with Vanburn Holder for the ninth wicket and 64 with last man Andy Roberts as the West Indies won by a wicket in the final over.

Elsewhere, an improved Sri Lanka scored 276/4 against Australia despite two of their batsmen being sent to hospital by Jeff Thomson's short-pitched pace bowling. Nevertheless, they still fell 52 runs short of victory. In Group A, England beat New Zealand by 80 runs while India crushed East Africa by ten wickets.

The final round of group matches saw England thrash East Africa by 196 runs to seal top spot in Group A while Turner hit another century for New Zealand as the Kiwis saw off India by four wickets to clinch second place.

In Group B, a sell-out crowd at The Oval saw the West Indies bowl out Australia for 192. They then sealed a seven-wicket victory with 14 overs to spare to top the group with the losers already guaranteed the runner-up spot. Pakistan ended their tournament with a 192-run victory over Sri Lanka at Trent Bridge.

Australia's decision to bring in Gary Gilmour for the first semi-final against England proved crucial. The two sides met at Headingley on a grassy pitch that was criticised post-match by both captains.

Gilmour took 6-14 as England were all out for a paltry 93. In the run-chase, Australia collapsed to 39/6 before Gilmour partnered with Doug Walters to chase down the remaining runs.

In the other semi-final, New Zealand collapsed from 98/1 to 158 all out at The Oval. Alvin Kallicharran was the West Indies' top scorer for the second match in succession and his 72 underpinned a successful chase that concluded with five wickets and almost 20 overs to spare.

The final took place at Lord's on 21 June. Australia won the toss and put the West Indies in to bat, hoping to make use of the helpful early bowling conditions. Opener Roy Fredericks fell in dramatic fashion as he hooked Dennis Lillee for six only to then tread on his stumps to be dismissed hit wicket. Gordon Greenidge and Kallicharran then lost their wickets to Thomson and Gilmour respectively to leave the West Indies 50/3.

This brought skipper Clive Lloyd to the crease and he hit a century in a 149-run partnership with Rohan Kanhai. Lloyd took the game away from the Australians with 102 from 85 balls, including 12 fours and two sixes. Kanhai added a valuable 55 with important contributions coming lower down the batting order from Keith Boyce and Bernard Julien as the West Indies finished on 291/8.

Gilmour took 5-48 to back up his performance in the semi-finals and finish as the tournament's leading wicket-taker with 11 in just two matches.

The Australian innings turned on some brilliant fielding from Viv Richards, who ran out three of the top four batsmen. He dismissed Alan Turner with a direct hit from close range then Greg Chappell, who hesitated after a misfield. Then captain Ian Chappell went in similar fashion to his brother. Contributions from Doug Walters and Ross Edwards kept Australia in the hunt but they still required 59 runs to win off seven overs when the ninth wicket fell.

Amid chaotic scenes at the end, with West Indian fans running on to the pitch prematurely on several occasions, Murray ran out Thomson to seal a memorable 17-run victory. The West Indies were champions of the world.

West Indian journalist Tony Cozier described the first World Cup as, 'Perhaps the boldest and most ambitious innovation the game has known since the legalisation of overarm bowling.'

The first World Cup delivered with exciting cricket played in perfect conditions before the West Indies triumphed in a memorable final. Its success guaranteed its future as cricket's biggest international tournament.

31

The West Indies make Greig grovel
(1976)

THE WEST Indies' thrashing of England in the long, hot summer of 1976 marked the beginning of almost 20 years of domination over the world of cricket.

Although the tourists arrived in England as World Cup winners there were questions over their future. They had been soundly beaten in Australia following that triumph and were still rebuilding following the retirements of Garry Sobers, Rohan Kanhai and Lance Gibbs.

West Indies captain Clive Lloyd responded to the 5-1 defeat at the hands of Australia by transforming his bowling attack. His side had struggled to cope with the pace of Dennis Lillee and Jeff Thomson down under, so Lloyd decided to unleash an all-pace attack of his own, spearheaded by Michael Holding and Andy Roberts.

The series in England was given extra spice thanks to controversial comments made by the home captain Tony Greig.

Appearing on television to discuss the series, Greig said: 'I like to think that people are building these West Indians up, because I'm not really sure they're as good as everyone thinks they are.

'I'm not all that worried about them. I'm not really sure they're as good as everyone thinks. These guys, if they get on top they are magnificent cricketers. But if they're down, they grovel, and I intend, with the help of Closey [Brian Close] and a few others, to make them grovel.'

The remarks caused immediate uproar due to the racist connotations of the word 'grovel' being used in context with a team of black men, many of whom had slave ancestry.

Additionally, apartheid was a major issue at the time and Grieg was a South African playing for his adopted country due to the sporting isolation of his native land.

However, his comments served to both galvanise the opposition and also the tens of thousands of their supporters who flocked to grounds to see his words rammed back down his throat.

Lloyd said: 'The word "grovel" is one guaranteed to raise the blood pressure of any black man. The fact they were used by a white South African made it even worse. We were angry and West Indians everywhere were angry. We resolved to show him and everyone else that the days for grovelling were over.'

The West Indies dominated England over the following summer, winning both the Test and one-day series by 3-0 scorelines. Viv Richards smashed 829 runs in just four Tests, including two double centuries while Holding, Roberts, Vanburn Holder and Wayne Daniel unleashed a barrage of hostile pace bowling on the England batsmen.

The pace of the bowling attack quickened still further whenever Greig came in to bat. The England captain endured a miserable series, with the exception of the fourth Test, struggling for runs and wickets as his side was blown away.

The first Test at Trent Bridge was drawn despite Richards hitting 232 as the West Indies reached 494 in their first innings. England responded with a respectable 332, thanks largely to a David Steele century. The tourists then declared on 176/5 to set England a target of 339 and the home side reached 156/2 at the close on day five.

The second Test at Lord's was a low-scoring affair with a day's play lost to rain and it also ended in a draw.

The third Test is often remembered for Holding peppering an unprotected Close with unplayable deliveries that struck the opening batsman frequently and painfully on the body. That passage of play was in the final session of the third day as England began their second innings with a mountain to climb.

Despite bowling out the West Indies for 211, over half of which came from Gordon Greenidge's 132, England had been decimated by Holding's 5-17 and were all out for just 71 in their first innings.

In the second innings, Greenidge made his second century of the match while Richards hit 134. The West Indies declared on 411/5 leaving England with a mammoth target of 552 on a wearing, dry pitch that was perfect for fast bowling.

Although Close stood up to the pace barrage he was out for 20 and his opening partner John Edrich top-scored with 24 as England were all out for 126. Roberts took 6-37 as the tourists took a 1-0 lead in the series with a thumping 425-run victory.

The fourth Test at Headingley was closer thanks to first-innings centuries from Greig and wicketkeeper Alan Knott. However, England still fell short with Holding, Daniel and Roberts sharing the wickets in a 55-run win.

With their team leading 2-0, thousands of West Indies fans, many drawn from the large Caribbean population of south London, made the final Test at The Oval a virtual home match for the tourists.

The fans created a carnival atmosphere as their team batted for most of the first two days to score a monumental 687/8. This was underpinned by Richards' 291, his second double century of the series and highest Test score.

England responded with 435 thanks to a double century from Dennis Amiss but were still 252 runs behind as Holding took 8-92. Lloyd declined to enforce the follow-on, preferring to let openers Greenidge and Roy Fredericks pile on the misery for England with 182 quick runs in an unbeaten stand.

As England were made to suffer in the heat, the party continued in the stands. In response, Greig slowly walked towards the Harleyford Road side of the ground where the West Indies fans were congregated and dropped to his knees. As he grovelled to the crowd they responded to his gesture.

Greig said: 'I realise that I made a mistake in using that word at the start of the series and they haven't let me forget it.'

A target of 452 was always going to prove difficult for England to reach. Holding took another six wickets to finish with match figures of 14-149 as the home side were all out for 203.

West Indies won the match by 231 runs, and the Test series 3-0. The result confirmed the ascendency of the West Indies under Lloyd's captaincy. For almost 20 years the batting of Greenidge, Richards, Lloyd and others would combine with a battery of brilliant pace bowlers to sweep all before them.

32

The Packer circus comes to town
(1977)

KERRY PACKER'S World Series Cricket (WSC) was unveiled to a shocked cricket world in May 1977 and over the next two years it would change the game forever.

The launch of WSC split the cricketing world in two, particularly in Australia, and brought innovations both on and off the pitch. Cricketers were paid like other top sports stars for the first time, while the ways in which the sport was played, marketed and watched on television all changed permanently.

WSC brought with it, or hastened the advent of, day/night cricket, drop-in pitches, helmets, coloured clothing, television cameras at both ends of grounds and mass marketing for a television audience.

The revolution had its roots in Packer's failed 1976 bid to show Australian cricket on his commercial television station Channel Nine. Not only was the media magnate a cricket fan, but Australian sport counted as locally produced content, which he needed in order to meet a government-imposed quota for the channel.

Packer tabled a AUS$1.5m, three-year offer to the Australian Cricket Board (ACB) for the exclusive TV rights of cricket in Australia. Despite offering a sum eight times higher than that of the existing broadcaster, the Australian

Broadcasting Corporation, Packer was rebuffed as the ACB renegotiated a deal with the public broadcaster.

Packer was angry due to the manner in which his bid had been dismissed for an inferior bid without any opportunity for negotiation or bargaining, so decided to establish his own competition.

He said: 'Cricket is going to get revolutionised whether they like it or not. There is nothing they can do to stop me. Not a goddamn thing.

'Had I got those TV rights I was prepared to withdraw from the scene and leave the running of cricket to the board. I will take no steps now to help anyone. It's every man for himself and the devil take the hindmost.'

In late 1976, Packer began recruiting players with the help of recently retired Australian Test captain Ian Chappell. Negotiations continued behind the scenes at the Centenary Test in Melbourne in March 1977 by which time about two dozen players had committed to the new venture. England captain Tony Greig not only agreed to join the competition but to act as a recruiting agent in the English game.

By the time the Australian newspapers broke the story in May 1977, Packer had signed 35 of the world's top cricketers, including 13 of the 17-man Australian Ashes squad on tour in England at the time. There were also players from England, West Indies, Pakistan and South Africa (then banned from international matches because of apartheid).

As well as Greig, WSC also signed up Australian captain Greg Chappell and West Indies skipper Clive Lloyd. In addition, former Australia captain Richie Benaud was recruited to advise Packer on how to run WSC.

The reason that WSC was able to persuade so many top cricketers to sign up to an untested concept was purely and simply money. It offered a proper payday to cricketers who were being underpaid, even at the highest levels of the sport.

According to Packer, it was, 'the easiest sport in the world to take over ... nobody bothered to pay the players what they were worth'.

The cricket establishment reacted angrily to developments. Australia lost the Ashes 3-0 with a team that included their Packer players but those who had signed up to WSC were banned from all official cricket, including Sheffield Shield matches, for the Australian season of 1977/78. Greig was stripped of the England captaincy although he maintained his place in the team for the Ashes.

England also tried to ban Packer players, a matter which ended up in the High Court in London, when Greig, Mike Procter and John Snow brought a claim for restraint of trade.

The case took seven weeks and ended with Justice Slade finding that professional cricketers need to make a living and the International Cricket Conference (ICC) should not stand in their way simply because its own interests might be damaged.

The result landed the ICC and England's Test and County Cricket Board with massive legal fees. It also meant that Packer players could continue playing county cricket, even if they would no longer be selected for England.

Although Packer had triumphed in court, WSC was unable to describe its matches as Test matches, call one of its teams Australia or use the official Laws of Cricket. Unperturbed, WSC launched its own 'Super Tests', with teams including an Australian XI, a Rest of the World team and the West Indies.

WSC was also banned from using traditional cricketing venues and forced to use the stadia of other sports, notably Australian Rules football. This led to the development of drop-in pitches to ensure the right standard of playing strip. Pitches were grown in greenhouses and dropped into the surface by cranes.

The first season of Super Tests saw the World XI beat the Australian XI 2-1 and the West Indies beat the Australian team by the same margin. The World XI also claimed the one-day title.

However, WSC struggled to capture the imagination of the Australian sporting public during that first season. They were competing against a young, official team that beat India 3-2 in an exciting home series.

Those who played and watched WSC reported that the standard was high and the cricket hard. Australia's David Hookes suffered a broken jaw at the hands of a bouncer from West Indies paceman Andy Roberts in the second Super Test at the Sydney Showgrounds. This showed many fans how intense the WSC cricket was. It also led to the first helmets appearing on batters' heads.

The second season of WSC saw roles reversed as it gained in popularity while an inexperienced Australia Test side was hammered 5-1 in the 1978/79 Ashes series. WSC's move to day/night matches under floodlights proved a success. A crowd of 44,377 attended the first match of the 1978/79 International Cup, under the new floodlights at the Sydney Cricket Ground.

Although the Australian XI didn't win either the Super Tests or the International Cup it boasted household names like the Chappell brothers, Dennis Lillee and Rod Marsh making it the first choice of many Australian cricket fans rather than the struggling official team.

Meanwhile, shrinking Test crowds and mounting debts were taking their toll on the state cricket boards in Australia so, by May 1979, they were willing to negotiate with Packer, who finally got what he wanted. Channel Nine won the exclusive rights to broadcast Australian cricket on television. Packer was also granted a ten-year contract to promote and market the game through a new company, PBL Marketing.

WSC changed the game in many ways. First and foremost, cricket was forced to modernise itself and was transformed into a fully professional sport.

On the field, WSC innovations are now commonplace throughout the game. They include floodlit matches, coloured kit, white balls, fielding circles, helmets, drop-in pitches and motorised drinks carts.

Due to the punishing schedule, cricketers had to be fitter than ever before. They became full-time professionals and received better pay. Higher earnings were ensured through the sale of television rights, which has also given broadcasters a significant say in the running of the game.

Many of these changes may have happened eventually but it was the disruptive influence of the Packer circus that brought them about in such a short space of time.

33

Trevor Chappell bowls underarm
(1981)

Melbourne Cricket Ground, Melbourne, 1 February 1981
Third Final, World Series Cup

Australia	New Zealand
235/4	229/8
G. Chappell 90	Edgar 102
Snedden 2-52	G. Chappell 3-43

Australia won by six runs

TREVOR CHAPPELL'S underarm delivery of the final ball of a one-day international (ODI) match between Australia and New Zealand in 1981 remains one of the most notorious acts of bad sportsmanship ever to take place on a cricket pitch.

The act itself denied New Zealand a fair chance of snatching an unlikely tie with a six from the last ball of the match. Although the delivery was legal in Australia at the time, it was seen as being contrary to the spirit of cricket and caused widespread outrage. Fans, commentators and even the prime ministers of both countries all joined in the condemnation.

It also led to the ICC amending their regulations to outlaw underarm bowling to prevent such an incident from occurring again.

The incident happened on 1 February 1981 at the Melbourne Cricket Ground (MCG) in the third match in the best-of-five final of the 1980/81 World Series Cricket Cup. The series was tied 1-1, New Zealand having won the first match and Australia the second.

After winning the toss, Australian skipper Greg Chappell opted to bat and his unbeaten 90 helped his side to a total of 235/4 in tough batting conditions. The Australian innings wasn't without its own controversy though as Chappell appeared to be caught by Martin Snedden off the bowling of Lance Cairns when he was on 58.

Neither umpire saw Snedden's low catch and Chappell refused to take the fielder's word that it was clean. Television replays were clear with commentator Richie Benaud saying: 'There is no question in my mind that that was a great catch – clearly caught above the ground, a superb catch.'

However, television replays were not used for umpiring in 1981 and Chappell batted on for his 90.

The New Zealand reply started well with 42 from John Wright while his fellow opener Bruce Edgar finished the match with an unbeaten 102. As the match went into the final over the Kiwis were 221/6, still needing 15 to win the match with all-rounder Richard Hadlee on strike and Edgar at the other end.

Surprisingly, it was Trevor Chappell who bowled the last over as his brother had got his sums wrong and already bowled Dennis Lillee for his allotted ten overs.

Hadlee hit Trevor Chappell's first ball for four before perishing lbw to the second ball of the over. New Zealand wicketkeeper Ian Smith made a three-ball cameo, running two twice before seeing his middle stump cartwheel down the ground as he was clean bowled. This brought out Brian McKenchie to face the final ball needing to hit a six to tie the match.

In the event of a tie, under the rules of the time, the match would have been replayed.

Although the pitch was slow and a maximum seemed unlikely, Greg Chappell was concerned that McKenchie, who was a former All Black at rugby union, had the power to send the ball over the boundary. In response he decided to eliminate that possibility by asking his brother to bowl underarm, even though he knew it would not go down well.

He said: 'Quite honestly, I couldn't give a rat's tail. I was quite prepared for a rap over the knuckles if it saved us from the extra game.'

Bowling underarm was within the Laws of Cricket at the time, although it had been banned in some competitions. However, underarm bowling had long faded from use in senior cricket and was considered outdated and uncompetitive.

The umpires and batsmen were informed that the bowler was changing his delivery style and that the final ball would be delivered underarm. As the crowd realised what was happening they began to jeer while Australian wicketkeeper Rod Marsh warned the Chappells against going through with their plan and other fielders shook their heads.

Even commentator Ian Chappell, the elder brother of Greg and Trevor, was heard to shout from the back of the commentary box: 'No, Greg, no, you can't do that!'

Regardless of the building furore, Trevor Chappell rolled the ball along the pitch to McKechnie. The batsman blocked it and immediately threw his bat skyward in disgust. McKechnie later said he thought about trying to slog it but didn't want to be embarrassed by getting bowled.

The New Zealand batsmen walked off the field in disgust. The New Zealand captain, Geoff Howarth, ran on to the field to plead with the umpires. Howarth believed underarm bowling to be illegal in the competition, as per the rules of other one-day tournaments at the time. The umpires told him the delivery was legal.

Inside the Kiwi dressing room, a tea cup was smashed against the wall while Benaud described it on television as 'one of the worst things I have ever seen done on a cricket field'.

After the incident, the Prime Minister of New Zealand, Robert Muldoon, described it as: 'The most disgusting incident I can recall in the history of cricket ... it was an act of true cowardice and I consider it appropriate that the Australian team were wearing yellow.'

Malcolm Fraser, the Australian Prime Minister, called it 'contrary to all the traditions of the game'.

As a direct result of the incident, underarm bowling was banned by the ICC as 'not within the spirit of the game'.

Greg Chappell later confessed to feeling tired and stressed after a long, demanding Australian cricket season. He had also been on the field at the MCG for most of the match, which had been played on a sweltering summer's day.

The Australian skipper said he wasn't aware of how badly his decision had been received until he was walking off the ground. He later told a documentary: 'The kids started jumping the fence and running out and this young girl tugged on my shirtsleeve. And I looked down at her, and she was looking up at me and she said: "You cheated." At that moment, I'd thought that this might be a bit bigger than I'd even imagined.'

34

India win the World Cup *(1983)*

Lord's, London, 25 June 1983
World Cup Final

India	West Indies
183 (54.4 overs)	140 (52 overs)
Krishnamachari Srikkanth 38	Viv Richards 33
Andy Roberts 3/32	Mohinder Amarnath 3/12
India won by 43 runs	

INDIA'S JOURNEY to cricketing superpower was a long one that started in the 1930s and proceeded at a glacial pace for many years. It took almost two decades for the side to register their first ever Test victory and another 20 years before it produced a team with enough quality to challenge the top teams regularly.

The blue touchpaper was truly lit on India's ascent when they sprung one of the biggest shocks in cricket history by overcoming the all-conquering West Indies to win their first World Cup.

By their own admission India did not expect to compete seriously in the tournament, let alone win the final against the two-time champions. The holders had not lost a World Cup match in the first two editions. By contrast, India had won one match out of six in the previous two tournaments, which was against lowly East Africa.

Indian batsman Sandeep Patil said: 'India were nowhere in contention. The team had hardly performed well in the previous two editions. So, as we left India, virtually all of us were in a holiday mood. Cricket was not the first thing on our minds.

'More than thinking about facing Malcolm Marshall, Bob Willis and Jeff Thomson, we were engrossed in planning our sightseeing activities. After getting to London, we were excited to see Buckingham Palace, Hyde Park and Trafalgar Square.'

India served up a warning of what was to come in their opening group as they comfortably saw off the West Indies by 34 runs at Old Trafford. Yashpal Sharma's 89 helped the side to a total of 262 in 60 overs. In response, West Indies were bundled out for 228, with Ravi Shastri and Roger Binny picking up three wickets each.

India made it two wins out of two by defeating Zimbabwe in their next game. All-rounder Madan Lal took 3-27 with wicketkeeper Syed Kirmani claiming five catches as Zimbabwe were restricted to 155. In reply, a 79-run partnership between Mohinder Amarnath and Patil guided India to a comfortable five-wicket victory.

However, India were to lose their next two matches by wide margins, putting them at risk of another early exit from a World Cup tournament.

Australia thrashed them by 162 runs with Trevor Chappell scoring 110 off 131 balls as his side reached 320/9 from their 60 overs. India wilted under the pressure of the imposing total as they were skittled for just 158 with medium-pacer Ken MacLeay taking 6-39.

In the rematch with the West Indies, Viv Richards' century helped his side to a total of 282 before the fast bowlers went to work. India were pegged back by the loss of early wickets and Dilip Vengsarkar was forced to retire hurt after being hit in the mouth by Malcolm Marshall. Only four Indian batsmen reached double figures as they were bowled out for 216.

The two defeats put a huge dent in India's hopes of progressing to the semi-finals; they simply had to win their final two group games to survive. Those hopes were soon hanging by a thread as the team were reduced to 9/4 by Zimbabwe in Tunbridge Wells.

That brought captain Kapil Dev out to bat and the skipper proceeded to rescue his side with one of the great World Cup innings. Dev hit a stunning 175 not out from just 138 balls, a knock that contained 16 fours and six sixes.

At the time, it was the highest individual score in ODI cricket, and with Kirmani, Dev put together the then highest partnership for the ninth wicket in ODIs with a stand of 126.

India finished on 266/8, which set up a 31-run victory as Zimbabwe failed to chase it down.

This lifted India for their final group match, which was a virtual knockout tie against Australia. After posting a total of 247, India's pace trio of Lal, Binny and Balwinder Sandhu proved too much for the Australians, who were all out for 129.

India were through to the semi-finals where they would face England. The hosts were favourites after topping their group with five wins. England won the toss as Old Trafford and opted to bat first. They were apparently cruising at 141/3 before Amarnath produced a match-changing spell that stemmed the flow of runs as well as removing David Gower and Mike Gatting. From a promising position England were all out for a disappointing 213.

An opening-wicket stand of 46 put India on course to reach the target. Amarnath added 46, securing the Man of the Match award in the process, before half-centuries from Yashpal Sharma and Patil got India across the line with more than five overs to spare.

Through to the final for the first time, the Indian team would face the West Indies for the third time in the tournament. The West Indies were aiming to win the World Cup for the third time in a row and were heavy favourites with the bookmakers.

India lost the toss and were put in to bat by Clive Lloyd. On a green wicket that looked like it would favour the bowlers they faced a fearsome line-up of Andy Roberts, Joel Garner, Michael Holding and Marshall.

After the loss of Sunil Gavaskar for just 2, Krishnamachari Srikkanth and Amarnath took the score past 50 before the former was trapped lbw by Marshall. Dev scored 15 before being caught off the bowling of Larry Gomes as the West Indies bowlers all picked up wickets. Resistance by the Indian tail saw Lal, Kirmani and Sandhu all reach double figures and the tenth wicket add 22 runs.

A score of 183 all out looked easily achievable for the champions but Dev refused to concede defeat. He said: 'Team, if this is not a winning total, then it's definitely a fighting total.'

Spurred on by their captain's bullishness, the Indian bowling exploited the weather and pitch conditions perfectly. Sandhu clean bowled Greenidge for just 1 before Desmond Haynes and Viv Richards took the score to 50. Richards looked to be in excellent form as he threatened to take the game away from India with seven boundaries.

Three of those boundaries came off a single Lal over but the all-rounder hit back taking the wickets of Haynes, Richards and Gomes to leave the West Indies reeling at 66/4. Binny removed Lloyd cheaply before Jeff Dujon and Marshall put on 43 for the seventh wicket. Amarnath dismissed them both and after Dev had trapped Andy Roberts lbw, he took the last wicket of Holding.

The West Indies had been bowled out for 140 from 52 overs, sealing India's victory by 43 runs and completing one of the most stunning upsets in cricket history. It still remains the lowest ever total successfully defended in a World Cup Final.

Lloyd, the defeated captain, said: 'Indian cricket has arrived. And it's here to stay.'

The trophy was much more than just silverware for India. The sight of Dev lifting the World Cup trophy on the Lord's balcony not only brought joy to the team's legions of supporters but inspired future generations of Indian cricketers.

35

AB takes over as Australia captain
(1984)

WHEN ALLAN Border took over as Australian captain in November 1984 the nation's cricket team was at a historically low ebb.

The fallout from World Series Cricket continued to have a negative impact on cricket in Australia and Test results had been so poor that Border's predecessor Kim Hughes had resigned in tears.

When Border retired from the role in 1994 he left his successor Mark Taylor a side on the cusp of global domination. The West Indies were beaten the following year and Australia became the pre-eminent team in world cricket for the rest of the decade and well into the 21st century.

At the end of his playing career Border held the records for most Tests played with 156, 153 of them consecutively, and runs with 11,174. His 93 Test matches as a captain was also a record, as was his 156 catches for a non-wicketkeeper.

Border's place as one of the great Australian Test captains is assured – he led the team from the dark days of the early 1980s to the start of a golden era. However, that journey was far from straightforward and the early years of Border's captaincy were filled with setbacks and challenges on and off the pitch.

Border, who was often known as AB or Captain Grumpy, did not feel he was a natural leader and came reluctantly to the captaincy. Australia were 2–0 down to the West Indies when he was appointed and his first Test as captain ended in a heavy defeat to Clive Lloyd's all-conquering side. Although the series was lost Border did manage to lead the team to a draw and a victory in the final two Tests of the Australian summer.

However, Border's hopes of leading a successful Ashes tour were dealt a heavy blow in April 1985. Seven of the players originally selected for the tour defected to join a rebel tour of apartheid South Africa instead. Border would eventually forgive the players involved but never forgot.

Border later said: 'I felt very let down. We were playing in Sharjah and everyone was having a beer and saying that the team was starting to get it together. There was that sort of talk. You feel such a fool when you then read in the paper that blokes you have trusted, who have told you how great the future looks, are going to South Africa.'

Although Border led from the front with his batting in the following series, Australia were comprehensively beaten 3-1 by England. Border hit 196 at Lord's where Australia were victorious and scored an unbeaten 146 at Old Trafford to salvage a draw in the fourth Test.

There was little improvement over the following southern hemisphere summer. Australia were defeated in a Test series for the first time by New Zealand and were then dominated by India in a drawn series. In the second Test against India it was Border's second-innings 163 that staved off defeat as he scored over half his side's runs. Two more centuries followed for the captain when the team travelled to New Zealand but once again this was not enough to prevent his side falling to defeat as the Kiwis held on to the Trans-Tasman Trophy.

Crucially, the former Australian captain Bobby Simpson joined the team as an observer in New Zealand. He was appointed Australia cricket coach shortly afterwards and his partnership with Border was vital in restoring the team's fortunes.

A drawn series in India was remarkable for the first Test ending in a tie, only the second match to finish that way in history, with Border scoring another century.

The tied Test showed both Border's man-management skills and hard edge as he goaded a sick and dehydrated Dean Jones into playing on and scoring a superb double hundred rather than retiring hurt.

A home Ashes defeat to England followed and despite winning the final match in that series, Australia were left with only three wins from 23 Test matches.

However, the team's unexpected victory in the 1987 Cricket World Cup proved to be a turning point and heralded the start of more prosperous times.

Despite starting the tournament as outsiders Australia defeated hosts and defending champions India by one run in the opening match. Four further wins over New Zealand and Zimbabwe saw Australia progress to the semi-finals where they saw off co-hosts Pakistan by 18 runs.

They met England in the final and David Boon's 75 gave them the platform to set a target of 253. Border chipped in with a vital 31 runs from 31 balls and then made a crucial intervention during England's chase. With Bill Athey and England captain Mike Gatting compiling a threatening-looking stand the Australian skipper brought himself on to bowl against his counterpart. Gatting lost his wicket as he was caught off an ill-judged reverse sweep as Australia clinched the trophy with a seven-run victory.

The following Australian season saw the team take its first Test series victory in four years. New Zealand were beaten 1-0 while Border recorded his highest Test score of 205 and passed Greg Chappell as Australia's highest run-scorer. The Bicentennial Test against England at Sydney was drawn, then Australia won their inaugural home Test match against Sri Lanka. Border's contribution for the five Tests was 426 runs at 71.00 average.

There were further setbacks with a lost series in Pakistan in 1988 and another home defeat to the West Indies the following season. Although Border's batting suffered in the 3-1 loss to the West Indies the sole Australian victory came in the fourth Test where he took 11-96.

Previously, he had taken 16 wickets in 99 Tests and receiving the player of the match award, Border said: 'There will be batsmen all around the world shaking their heads in disbelief when they see the result.'

However, the 1989 Ashes tour was a watershed for the Australian team as the form of new opener Taylor, a formidable bowling unit and a new, tougher attitude from the skipper combined to achieve Border's first major series win as a Test captain.

Australia won 4-0, their first victory in a Test series abroad since 1977 and best result in England since the Invincibles' tour of 1948. The result came after Border consciously fashioned a more aggressive approach to the captaincy.

He said: 'I made a personal choice to have a harder edge as captain, be more stand-offish towards them [the English] ... It was a hard thing to do and they all got the shits, but it was all part and parcel of what I wanted to achieve.'

He was subsequently named the 1989 Australian of the Year for his part in helping Australia regain the Ashes.

Further series victories came against Pakistan and Sri Lanka before a successful defence of the Ashes saw a 3-0 win in the 1990/91 season.

A win against the West Indies remained elusive though and hopes were high going into the 1991 tour of the Caribbean. However, after a good start, Australia's performances tailed off, and the West Indies won 2-1.

This was followed by a 4-0 win over India in Australia and a 1-0 win in Sri Lanka in 1992, Border's only series victory on the subcontinent as captain.

In between those series victories a disappointing 1992 World Cup saw Australia, host and holders, knocked out in the group stage.

Border was firmly focused on beating the West Indies, who toured Australia in 1992/93 in a rebuilding phase. Shane Warne bowled the team to victory in the second Test and Australia held a 1-0 lead going in to the fourth Test in Adelaide.

They came within one run of victory before last man Craig McDermott was given out. The batting then wilted to Curtly Ambrose on a fast pitch in Perth in the deciding Test. Border's failure to defeat the West Indies was the biggest disappointment of his career. He retired one year before it was finally achieved.

There was consolation with a personal milestone as Border passed Gavaskar's record for the most Test runs whilst on tour in New Zealand.

A third Ashes tour as captain saw Australia dominate as Warne's emergence helped the tourists run out convincing 4-1 winners. The Australians then claimed the Trans-Tasman Trophy with a comfortable 2-0 victory over New Zealand at home in late 1993. Border scored 105 in the third Test on his home ground at Brisbane. It was the last of his 27 Test centuries.

Border ended his career by leading the first Australian team to play a Test series against South Africa in 1994 after their return to international cricket. Three Tests were played in each country, and both series ended 1-1.

Over almost a decade and 93 matches at the helm Border re-established the credibility of Australian cricket. He helped rebuild the team, first making them hard to beat, then turning them into World Cup and Ashes winners. The side he left behind proved capable of dominating the cricketing stage for years to come.

36

Graeme Hick scores 1,000 runs before the end of May *(1988)*

ONLY EIGHT batsmen have scored 1,000 first-class runs before the end of May in the English cricket season. They include some of the greatest names in the sport of cricket including W.G. Grace, Don Bradman and Wally Hammond.

Grace was the first man to achieve the feat as he enjoyed an Indian summer in 1885 while Bradman is the only one to do it more than once. He first did it in 1930 and once again eight years later. The milestone was reached seven times between Grace becoming the first and Bill Edrich joining Bradman in 1938, a span of 53 years. Since then it has become a far harder total to reach with only two batsmen managing it since the Second World War.

Both played for Worcestershire with Kiwi Glenn Turner reaching the 1,000 in 1973 and Graeme Hick joining this exclusive club in 1988.

There are several reasons it has become more difficult for modern batsmen to score 1,000 first-class runs before the end of May.

Partly it is due to changes to the cricketing calendar with fewer first-class matches scheduled for English county teams and touring international teams and more limited-overs competitions taking their place.

Another complication is presented by the removal of first-class status from the counties' matches against various university sides. In the past this might present the chance of some easy runs before facing county and international bowlers.

In addition, the English weather cannot be relied upon to help batsmen in their quest either. The English cricket season starts in April, a month synonymous with showers, and May is far from guaranteed to be dry. Matches are often affected by rain or even, on rare occasions, delayed because of snow. This means that overs, sessions and days can be lost and, in extreme cases, matches abandoned.

Even if the rain stays away the contest between bat and ball often favours the ball early in the English season. Bowlers are helped by damp pitches, where the ball is more likely to behave unexpectedly, as they are yet to harden under prolonged sunshine. In addition, overcast conditions are helpful to swing bowlers, particularly in morning sessions.

Hick was the last man to overcome these hurdles and prove the challenge could be met in the modern era.

The Zimbabwe-born batsman arrived at New Road from Harare in 1984 and two years later became the youngest player in history to score 2,000 first-class runs in an English season.

In 1988, his season got off to a flying start with 410 runs coming in April alone, a record for the month that stood until Warwickshire's Ian Bell scored 480 in April 2005. Over half of those runs came at Old Trafford, where Hick flayed the Lancashire attack for 212. He finished the month with scores of 86 and 14 against Nottinghamshire in Worcester.

In the first week of May he made his highest first-class score with an epic innings of 405 not out against Somerset at Taunton. The score was made on a good pitch, although Hick arrived at the crease with his team in trouble after they had subsided to 132/5.

Hick gave the bowling side a couple of early chances and was dropped in the gully on 148. However, he was largely imperious as he batted with the Worcestershire tail to record the biggest score seen in county cricket since Lancashire's Archie MacLaren had flogged the same opponents for 425 in 1895.

This score meant that by 6 May 1988, Hick had already collected 815 runs for the campaign, making his 1,000 before the end of the month seem almost inevitable.

However, his proximity to the target combined with the quadruple century served to raise the youngster's profile. Hick became the centre of media attention with cameras trained on each innings. For a time, the pressure seemed to get to him and a series of batting failures followed, including twice to Somerset at New Road.

This mini slump left Hick requiring 153 from his final match in May to make history. However, he would have to tame the lethal pace attack of the touring West Indies team, featuring Curtly Ambrose, Courtney Walsh, Patrick Patterson and Ian Bishop to achieve his goal.

Just five days after celebrating his 22nd birthday, a hugely impressive innings saw Hick reach his target on the first day of play. He scored 172 not out against the tourists to reach a total of 1,019 runs before the end of May.

Hick scored a career-best aggregate of 2,713 runs in the 1988 season. This included ten first-class centuries, as he helped Worcestershire to their fourth County Championship title.

He was also named Player of the Year by the Professional Cricketers' Association and won the Walter Lawrence

Trophy for the fastest century of the season, scored in 79 balls against Surrey.

Despite these individual and team accolades it is the 1,000 runs before the end of May that is most remembered about Graeme Hick's summer of 1988.

Since then, entry to the 1,000 runs club remains elusive. West Indies great Brian Lara came close to emulating Hick during his run fest of 1994 and Rob Key passed 1,000 on 2 June in 2004.

Nick Compton came closest to achieving 1,000 runs before the end of May in 2012 only to be foiled by the weather. He needed 59 runs on 31 May against Worcestershire. Rain intervened with Compton having only scored 9, but he scored a century after resuming his innings the following day to pass 1,000 runs on 1 June.

Until a batsman starts the season with the required combination of skill, form, fixtures and weather, Hick will remain the last man to score 1,000 first-class runs before the end of May in an English cricket season.

The 1,000 Club

1885 – W.G. Grace
1900 – Tom Hayward
1927 – Wally Hammond
1928 – Charlie Hallows
1930 – Don Bradman
1938 – Don Bradman and Bill Edrich
1973 – Glenn Turner
1988 – Graeme Hick

The first English team to tour overseas, on board their ship to North America, 1859. Standing at left Robert Carpenter, William Caffyn, Tom Lockyer; middle row John Wisden, HH Stephenson, George Parr, James Grundy, Julius Caesar, Thomas Hayward, John Jackson; front row Alfred Diver, John Lillywhite.

Engraving from 1770 showing underarm bowling, a curved bat, two stumps and the score being kept on a carved stick.

Engraving from 1777 showing a cricket match at Hambledon.

William Clarke, founder of the All-England XI.

Bernard Bosanquet, the first bowler to master the googly, in a Vanity Fair *cartoon.*

A Harold Larwood delivery strikes Bert Oldfield a chilling blow on the head at the Adelaide Oval.

John Holt and Everton Weekes walk out to bat against England in the first Test of the 1954 series at Sabina Park in Kingston, Jamaica.

England captain Len Hutton tosses the coin, watched by Australia captain Lindsay Hassett.

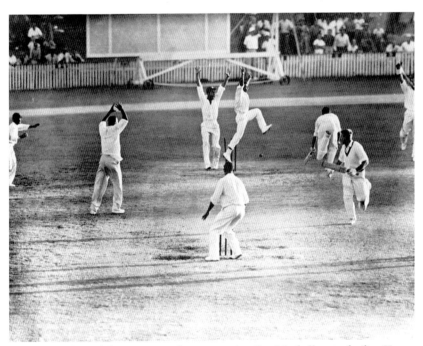

The West Indies celebrate as Joe Solomon runs out Ian Meckiff to tie the first Test in Brisbane.

Basil D'Oliveira celebrates being selected for England in 1966.

England celebrate taking the wicket of Australian captain Bill Lawry in the first ever one-day international. Melbourne, 1971.

Tony Greig and Kerry Packer at a World Series Cricket press conference in London.

Trevor Chappell bowls the final ball of the match underarm, 1981.

Clive Lloyd on his way to a century in the 1975 World Cup Final.

Fans stream on to the pitch to celebrate India's win in the 1983 World Cup Final.

Graeme Hick on his way to 172 against the West Indies and 1,000 runs before the end of May 1988.

Allan Border celebrates winning the 1989 Ashes 4-0.

Shane Warne in action against England, Old Trafford 1993.

Mahendra Singh Dhoni prepares for action in the 2008 Indian Premier League. Dhoni was the most expensive player at the league's first auction.

New Zealand's Kane Williamson and Ross Taylor celebrate victory in the inaugural World Test Championship.

37

Tendulkar confirms his talent with Old Trafford ton *(1990)*

Old Trafford, Manchester, 9–14 August 1990
Second Test

England	India
519	432
Atherton 131	Azharuddin 179
Hirwani 4-174	Fraser 5-124
320/4 dec	343/6
Lamb 109	Tendulkar 119 not out

Match drawn

INDIA'S SACHIN Tendulkar is widely regarded as one of the greatest batsmen to have ever played the game of cricket. His international career lasted almost quarter of a century and the 'Little Master' collected many records, awards and plaudits along the way.

Tendulkar scored 100 international centuries during his career as well as scoring the most runs and making the most appearances in both Tests and one-day internationals (ODIs). *Wisden* rated him the second-greatest Test batsman of all time, behind only the great Don Bradman, and the second-greatest ODI batsman of all time, with only West Indies legend Viv Richards ahead of him in that format.

Few of the runs he made during his career were more important than his first Test match century, scored against England when he was just 17 years old. Not only did Tendulkar bat with great maturity to save the Test for India; he also confirmed his potential as a future great of the game.

A child prodigy, Tendulkar's schoolboy years had been marked by phenomenal run-scoring feats with hundreds, double hundreds and even triple hundreds scored regularly. As he moved into the professional ranks he added centuries on debut in both the Ranji and Irani trophies.

He became India's youngest-ever Test debutant when he toured Pakistan as a 16-year-old in 1989. Expectations were high that he would break Mushtaq Mohammad's record as the youngest-ever century-maker.

Tendulkar made 15 in his first Test innings before being bowled by Waqar Younis, who was also making his debut in the match. He made two half-centuries later in the series and earned plaudits for his bravery but a hundred proved elusive.

A few months later he came closer to the landmark during the second Test against New Zealand in Napier. He was unbeaten on 80 overnight but could only add eight runs before being caught at mid-off as he attempted to drive Danny Morrison.

That made it seven Tests without a hundred and Mushtaq's record was safe as Tendulkar would have passed 17 years and 82 days by the time the Test series in England started the following July.

On their 1990 tour to England, India found themselves in the middle of a summer of runs. The first Test saw six hundreds in all, including a mammoth 333 from England captain Graham Gooch, but Tendulkar was not amongst the centurions. Amidst this mountain of runs he scored 10 and 27.

India lost the Test despite scoring 454 in their first innings, which was lit up by Mohammad Azharuddin's 121. The Indian captain's knock is rated as one of the best centuries scored by an overseas batsman at Lord's. Meanwhile, Kapil Dev hit Eddie Hemmings for four sixes to avoid the follow-on. These heroics proved in vain as England took a 1-0 lead to Manchester for the second Test.

Now at Old Trafford, India needed to keep the series alive, while Gooch tried to avoid another run fest by asking the groundsman for a quick and bouncy wicket. However, a bout of cold weather put paid to those plans.

Gooch hit his third hundred in as many innings as he put on 225 with his opening partner, Mike Atherton, who also scored a hundred. Robin Smith then rubbed salt into India's wounds with a blistering 121 as England made 519.

India hit back with 432 in their first innings. Azharuddin was once again the star turn with 179 while Sanjay Manjrekar fell short of his century with 93. Tendulkar came in with the innings on a knife-edge and took almost an hour to get off the mark. Once the runs started flowing he began to showcase the strokeplay that would be a feature of his batting in the years to come.

Tendulkar fell to Hemmings on 68 but his vital runs helped India to limit the first-innings deficit and remain competitive in the match. More importantly, it provided a confidence boost that he could handle English conditions and set up him up for the second innings.

England continued to pile on the runs in their second innings. Allan Lamb scored a century for the hosts with Atherton adding 74. Smith hit a quick-fire 61 that allowed Gooch to declare 20 minutes into the final morning, leaving

India the improbable task of scoring 408 for victory – or surviving 90 overs for a draw on a wearing pitch.

Early wickets for Angus Fraser and Devon Malcolm saw India reduced to 35/2 before Manjrekar and Dilip Vengsarkar steadied the ship. However, the pair both perished to Hemmings after lunch with the score on 109, bringing Azharuddin and Tendulkar to the crease.

The Indian captain fell for just 11 as Hemmings struck again but Tendulkar played with a mixture of maturity, technical excellence and cricketing intelligence that belied his youth and inexperience at Test level.

Despite the precariousness of the match position Tendulkar took the attack to England, knocking the bowlers, particularly Hemmings – who dropped a caught and bowled chance when he was on just 10 – out of their stride. When Gooch set attacking fields, Tendulkar cleared them with chipped shots. As England became more defensive he continually pierced the field with cover drives to keep the runs coming.

Tendulkar put on 56 with Dev before a stand of 160 with Manoj Prabhakar secured the draw. Finally, he reached three figures with a cover drive off Fraser to become the second-youngest Test centurion at 17 years and 107 days old.

Tendulkar said: 'When I passed 90, it was obvious that the thought of scoring a hundred would start to affect me. After all, it would be my first international century and the crowd had already started expecting it from me.

'I reminded myself of what had happened in New Zealand and was conscious not to repeat the same mistake. There was still some time left in the day's play and England could press for victory if I got out.

'The crowd stood to applaud but I was extremely uncomfortable about acknowledging them. I had never been in that position before and was acutely embarrassed about raising my bat to the stadium.'

The innings drew praise from many quarters, including the England captain.

Gooch said: 'He had great balance, he moved his feet backward and forward. He had a good head position, good timing, and the time to play his shots. He never looked ruffled. And he had a good temperament. So all the important skills you need to be a big run-maker were there.'

The innings confirmed that Tendulkar was on the road to stardom with a glittering career ahead of him. By the time he retired he had added another 99 international centuries and over 34,000 runs in Tests and ODIs. He was part of the Indian team that won the 2011 Cricket World Cup and won a host of individual awards to become one of the greatest batsmen ever to grace the game of cricket.

38

South Africa versus England, World Cup semi-final *(1992)*

Sydney Cricket Ground, Sydney, 22 March 1992

World Cup semi-final

England	**South Africa**
252/5	232/6 (43 overs)
Graeme Hick 83	Andrew Hudson 46
Meyrick Pringle 2-36	Richard Illingworth 2-46

England won by 19 runs (revised target)

THE 1992 Cricket World Cup was memorable for a host of reasons, including Pakistan's run from the brink of elimination to champions. It was also the first World Cup to be held in Australia and saw the long-delayed debut of South Africa at the tournament.

For the first time the competition featured coloured kits, floodlights and white balls. It also saw the debut of a new rain rule, which went on to play a major role in the farcical finish to one of the semi-finals.

Pakistan won the World Cup despite almost going out in the round robin stage. Imran Khan's 'Cornered Tigers' lost three of their first five matches, and may have lost a fourth after collapsing to a meagre total of 74 against England before the match was lost to rain. The point gained from that no-result proved crucial as Pakistan won their final three group matches to squeeze into the semis. They then beat fancied New Zealand and England sides to become world champions.

South Africa finally took part in a World Cup, following the end of apartheid and the country's readmission to international sport after long years of exile.

The Proteas lit up the tournament with the lightning fast bowling of Allan Donald and electric fielding of Jonty Rhodes. Victories over Australia, West Indies, Pakistan, India and Zimbabwe carried them all the way to the semi-finals.

Then in the semi-final at the Sydney Cricket Ground (SCG) the team required 22 runs from their last 13 deliveries to beat England and reach the final before rain intervened.

What followed not only set the tone for South Africa's World Cup exits, which have since veered between the absurd and the ridiculous, but paved the way for the introduction of the Duckworth–Lewis rule that has since held the key to revising totals when overs are lost.

The new rain rule was intended to rebalance the system to take the advantages of chasing into account. Previously totals were revised by working out the runs-per-over of the first innings and then deducting that for each over lost by the side batting second. This tended to disadvantage the side batting first as they would have been pacing their innings for a full allocationt of overs.

The solution, drawn up by experts including Richie Benaud, was that when rain interrupted the second innings of a match the reduction in the target was to be proportionate to the lowest-scoring overs of the side batting first.

The first inkling of the problems inherent in the new system were apparent in England's round robin match against Pakistan. England bowled out Pakistan for 74 in Adelaide before three hours were lost to rain. As only Pakistan's most productive 16 overs were included in the total, England found themselves chasing 64 runs in their 16 overs. That target presented England with a far stiffer target than their bowling effort had merited and they still needed 40 from eight overs when rain intervened again. On this occasion play was abandoned and the points shared.

Perhaps that should have served as a warning to Kepler Wessels as he prepared to meet England in the semi-final at the SCG. However, the South African skipper won the toss and elected to field first despite rain in the air and a grim forecast.

The decision was questioned by Channel Nine's Ian Chappell, who asked: 'Kepler, not too worried about the rain?'

Wessels replied: 'Yeah, it is a calculated risk ... if it rains and we are bowling, it is not too bad. The problem comes if you are batting tonight and it rains, but that is a risk we are prepared to take.'

England scored 252/6 in their 45 overs with Graeme Hick scoring a crucial 83. However, the innings was shortened as South Africa had bowled their overs too slowly and incurred a fine.

A steady South African run chase started slowly but picked up pace with Rhodes' 43 from 38 balls. With five overs remaining Brian McMillan and Dave Richardson were at the crease and they needed 47 to win as the rain grew heavier.

The umpires, Brian Aldridge and Steve Randell, consulted and then spoke to the players. The South Africa batsmen were happy to carry on while England skipper Graham Gooch wanted to come off. The umpires agreed with Gooch that conditions were unfit and the players were taken from the field.

Crucially, any time lost would result in overs being deducted, and under competition rules those would be the least productive for the side batting first. South Africa had bowled two maiden overs in England's innings, which meant that with 2.1 overs remaining any time lost would not result in a reduction in the target but would mean South Africa had fewer balls in which to score the runs.

When the rain stopped the total time lost was 12 minutes. It was announced that one over had been deducted and South Africa's new target was 22 from seven balls, prompting jeers from the 35,000 crowd. However, the truth was even worse. Errors had been made and the target was revised once again to an impossible 22 from just one ball.

McMillan took an easy single off the bowling of Chris Lewis and headed back to the pavilion with a face like thunder. South Africa did, however, return to the field to shake hands with the England players and do a lap of honour around the SCG. Wessels refused to blame his opponents for the loss, despite elements of the crowd doing so.

He said: 'If I'd been in Graham's position I'd have done the same thing. We had to bowl through semi-hard rain in their innings and didn't come off but England did. That's the umpires' decision. I can't do anything about this. I don't blame Gooch. It's unfortunate the England players got booed because it was no fault of theirs. It's just the rules.'

Wessels' part in the defeat certainly set the tone for South Africa's subsequent tournament exits. In 1999, Lance Klusener and Donald contrived a comical run-out when they only needed one run from four balls to beat Australia in the World Cup semi-final. Four years later, on home soil, the team miscalculated what was required from a run chase after a rain delay in Durban. And in 2011 it was the needless run-out of A.B. de Villiers, the best batsmen in the world at the time, with less than five an over required that cost them.

The 1992 semi-final had a more lasting legacy, the introduction of the Duckworth–Lewis method. This replaced the Average run rate method, which skewed matches to the chasing team and the most productive overs method, which had tended to favour the team batting first.

The Duckworth–Lewis method takes into account both the number of overs that are still to be bowled and the number of wickets the chasing team have in hand. It uses these resources to calculate a total that changes every time a wicket falls.

Although the formula is considered too complex by some, scoreboards often now show a Duckworth–Lewis par score. Both teams and spectators can see this score and easily understand how it relates to the match situation. Duckworth–Lewis is now an accepted part of the limited-overs landscape, but it only came into being after the debacle in Sydney in 1992.

39

The introduction of technology *(1992)*

ANDREW HUDSON'S run-out of Sachin Tendulkar in the first Test at Durban in 1992 was a close call. The umpire was unsure whether the batsman was out or not, so referred it to the third umpire, who sent Tendulkar back to the pavilion.

It was the first time technology had been used in a cricket match and set the game on the road to the sophisticated Decision Review System (DRS) that is so familiar in today's major matches.

India's 1992/93 tour of South Africa was historic in several ways. Not only was it India's first-ever visit to South Africa, but it was also the first series played in the country since their isolation due to apartheid had begun over 20 years earlier. It also saw the introduction of the International Cricket Council's (ICC) panel of neutral umpires.

Meanwhile, Omar Henry became the first non-white player to represent South Africa while captain Kepler Wessels became the first player to score centuries for two Test teams when he hit 118 in the first Test, having previously achieved the feat with Australia.

However, the lasting legacy of the tour was the decision of the United Cricket Board of South Africa to experiment with TV replays to settle difficult line decisions using a third umpire.

Following the run-out at Durban, Wessels said: 'I felt instantly the game had changed for ever – and for the better.'

Third umpire Karl Leibenberg made the first-ever DRS decision. It followed some sharp fielding by Jonty Rhodes, whose throw from backward point found Hudson and, despite being off balance, the short leg fielder managed to break the stumps before Tendulkar could make his ground.

Umpire Cyril Mitchley, who had helped trial the system, was 'almost certain' Tendulkar had been run out but referred the decision to be absolutely sure. The midwicket camera clearly showed Tendulkar was short of his ground and Liebenberg pressed the green light for go (which meant out). The decision had taken just 34 seconds longer than normal.

Wisden wrote: 'The tour will be remembered for the introduction of the ICC's scheme for independent umpires and even more for the South African cricket board's experiment using television replays to settle difficult line decisions. It was a successful innovation, welcomed by most players and officials after some initial reservations.

'Hitherto, for as long as the game has been played batsmen have received the benefit of an umpire's doubt. When officials on the field felt unable to decide, a third umpire in the pavilion watched video replays to rule on run-outs and stumpings (and hit-wicket decisions, though none arose).

'A green light signalled that the batsman must go, a red that he was not out. Invariably the crowd buzzed with excitement as they waited and at some grounds they were able to watch big-screen replays at the same time.'

Following the series, the cameras were fine-tuned in South African domestic cricket and became a permanent fixture. In time the technology evolved to become the DRS, which is now an accepted part of the game, with even umpires now acknowledging that their word is not always final.

The evolution from simple television replays continues to this day. The modern-day DRS reviews and corrects the on-field umpire's call through technologies including Ultra Edge, Hot Spot and Hawk-Eye, providing conclusive decisions.

Hawk-Eye is a ball-tracking system that was invented in 2001 to project the trajectory of the ball once delivered from the bowler's hand. It uses a number of cameras placed around the ground, or under the stadium roof, to generate a three-dimensional representation of the trajectory of the ball.

Hawk-Eye gives umpires a perspective on whether the ball has pitched and hit in line and would have gone on to hit the stumps to aid lbw decisions.

Ultra Edge is the latest advance in the Snickometer, or Snicko. Snicko produces a disturbance in a graph when the surface of the ball touches the bat or any other part of the batter. Ultra Edge uses a microphone, placed inside the stumps, as well as cameras around the ground, to detect the sound of the hit and determine the surface of the impact. The shape of the frequency helps the third umpire in making a conclusive decision on caught behind decisions.

Hot Spot uses an advanced infrared detection system to detect the heat signature of the ball's impact. It uses the camera on both ends of the ground and provides information based on the heat friction generated by a collision. Hot Spot helps umpires to judge the thinnest edges and close bat-pad lbw decisions.

And, in the modern game, Tendulkar's run-out might be confirmed by the use of LED bails.

All these technologies and their widespread usage in cricket matches confirm Wessels' view that the game had changed forever and for the better. Their accuracy and usefulness are now accepted by umpires, players and fans around the globe.

40

The Ball of the Century *(1993)*

Old Trafford, Manchester, 2–7 June 1993

First Ashes Test

Australia	England
289	210
Mark Taylor 124	Graham Gooch 65
Peter Such 6-67	Shane Warne 4-51
432/5 dec	332
Ian Healy 102	Graham Gooch 133
Peter Such 2-78	Shane Warne 4-86

Australia won by 179 runs

SHANE WARNE is now widely regarded as one of the greatest bowlers in cricket history but he was an unknown quantity when he arrived in England on the 1993 Ashes tour.

Warne proceeded to announce himself in dramatic fashion to Ashes contests and the wider cricketing world with a delivery that became known as 'The Ball of the Century'. The huge leg break claimed the scalp of England batsman Mike Gatting at Old Trafford and proved a pivotal moment in the first Ashes Test of 1993 and the series as a whole.

More significantly, the delivery signalled a revival of leg spin in world cricket, spearheaded by the irrepressible Warne, a bowler who would give batsmen around the globe nightmares for the next 14 years.

Warne had arrived in England for the 1993 Ashes with little fanfare. Prior to his arrival he had played in 11 Test matches and taken 31 wickets at a moderate average of 30.80 runs per wicket. Leg-spinners were a rarity in Test cricket at the time with Pakistan's Abdul Qadir almost single-handedly keeping the flame alive during the 1980s.

The Old Trafford pitch traditionally favoured spinners and England went into the first Test of the series with two spin bowlers, Phil Tufnell and Peter Such, in their side. However, Australia looked to be relying on their three-man pace attack with Warne as the sole spinner.

Australia were put in to bat by England captain Graham Gooch and made a modest 289 underpinned by a Mark Taylor century. In reply, England were 80/1 on the second day of the match when the Australian captain Allan Border tossed the ball to Warne.

After a short run-up Warne delivered a leg break to the right-handed Gatting. The ball drifted to the right and eventually pitched several inches outside the line of Gatting's leg stump. The batsman responded in textbook fashion by pushing his pad out to the pitch of the ball with his bat tucked in beside it and angled down for a forward defensive.

However, the ball landed in the bowlers' footmarks, which gave it extra turn and it spun past Gatting's defences and clipped the top of his off stump, removing the bail on the way through.

Commentating for television, former Australian captain Richie Benaud said: 'First ball in Test cricket in England for Shane Warne ... and he's done it. He's started off with the most beautiful delivery. Gatting has absolutely no idea what has happened to it, he still doesn't know. He asked [umpire] Kenny Palmer on the way out, Kenny Palmer just gave him a raised eyebrow and a little nod and that's all it needed.'

Gatting, who was known as a good player of spin bowling, said: 'It came down in a great area for him and it did spin an awfully long way from two or three inches outside leg stump.

'I stood there because I didn't hear the death rattle, then looked around and thought "blimey, there's a bail on the floor".

'My foot was in, so I knew I could not have been stumped. The ball had not brushed my bat, my glove or pad, so I thought Australia wicketkeeper Ian Healy must have kicked the bail off. It wasn't to be. The ball had clipped the bail and I had to go.'

Less charitably, Gooch said: 'He looked as though someone had just nicked his lunch. If it had been a cheese roll, it would never have got past him.'

The Ball of the Century, or Gatting Ball, reduced England to 80/2 and Warne removed Robin Smith just four runs later as Australia bowled out the hosts to earn a first-innings lead of 79.

That lead was extended as the tourists declared their second innings at 432/5. Warne then took another four wickets as Australia won the match by 179 runs, the spinner taking the Man of the Match award in the process.

The result of this match set the tone for the remainder of the series, and Australia cruised to a comfortable 4-1 victory, with Warne taking a total of 34 wickets at an average of 25.79 and being named Australia's Man of the Series.

The 1993 Ashes was a significant landmark on Australia's journey back to the top of world cricket. Their dominance of the game during the 1990s and 2000s dovetailed with the success of Warne. He won seven out of the eight Ashes series in which he played, contributing 40 wickets in a losing cause in 2005, and was a World Cup winner in 1999.

After bowling Gatting, Warne went on to become one of the greatest bowlers in cricket history, finishing with 708 Test wickets and a further 293 in one-day internationals.

Warne's bowling also showcased the skill, mystery and effectiveness of leg spin bowling after an era when pace bowling had dominated. He was at the forefront of a resurgence of popularity in the art of spin bowling in general, and leg spin in particular.

Warne said: 'The Ball of the Century was a fluke. It really was. I never did it again but I think it was meant to be. As a leg-spinner, you always try to bowl a perfect leg break every ball and I managed to do it first up. It sort of changed my whole life really on and off the field.

'I am proud that I have bowled it, especially to someone like Mike Gatting who was a fantastic player and the best player of spin in the England team. It was a very special moment.'

Warne may have said that the Ball of the Century changed his life, but its impact was felt far beyond. It launched a career that helped change cricket by contributing not only to his country's dominance of the sport but altering the way the game was played too.

41

MCC admits women members *(1998)*

THE MARYLEBONE Cricket Club's (MCC) vote to allow female members in 1998 was a landmark for the inclusion of women's cricket in the sport. It had taken 211 years, a high-profile and well-backed campaign and two votes, but women were finally to be allowed into the last male bastion of the game, the Lord's pavilion.

Although the MCC committee had first discussed admitting women as members in 1967 it wasn't until 1991 that the campaign began in earnest. That was the year that Rachael Heyhoe Flint applied for membership.

Heyhoe Flint had enjoyed a distinguished playing career, captaining England to victory in six Test series as well as the inaugural Women's Cricket World Cup (see Moment 29).

According to cricket journalist and former *Wisden* editor, Scyld Berry: 'She was, among other achievements, the Dr W.G. Grace of women's cricket – the pioneer without whom the game would not be what it is.'

Heyhoe Flint applied as 'R. Flint' in order to slip into the male-only application system but her form had an impressive list of signatures backing her application. These included the ex-Warwickshire and England batsman Dennis Amiss, cricket commentator Brian Johnston, lyricist Tim Rice and Wolverhampton businessman Sir Jack Hayward, who had helped fund the first Women's Cricket World Cup.

The identity of 'R. Flint' was swiftly revealed and her impressive cricket credentials ensured that the application caught the attention of those at the top of MCC. It also coincided with an appeal from Middlesex County Cricket Club to relax rules for the Lord's pavilion.

A recent change of policy at Lancashire's Old Trafford home had left Lord's as the only ground on the county circuit where the host county's female members could not enter their own pavilion.

Soon afterwards MCC took legal advice only to find that there was nothing in its rules to prevent a woman becoming a member. This was because the rules always referred to any 'person' who applied for membership and that gender of the applicant was never directly referred to.

The club had been a male preserve since 1787 and although the committee said women were welcome to apply, they also decided that there was a need for the existing members to support the move, support that was not forthcoming in 1991.

As the 1990s wore on this stance became more and more untenable. The Women's Cricket Association had merged into the new England and Wales Cricket Board, which was headquartered at Lord's.

Additionally, MCC's application to the Sports Council's Lottery Sports Fund to help pay for a new stand had been rejected on the specific grounds that the club did not admit women as members.

Then, in 1996, Colin Ingleby-Mackenzie, a long-standing supporter of women's membership, took on the presidency of MCC and led a two-year campaign to convince the membership to vote in favour of change. At the first attempt, in February 1998, the motion was carried, but by too slender a majority to change the club's rules.

However, that was not the end of the matter as Ingleby-Mackenzie forced a second vote the following September. This time a 70 per cent majority of members voted to allow female membership, ending 211 years of male exclusivity.

Heyhoe Flint was among a group of ten women who became honorary life members soon after the vote and in February 1999 five women were invited to join as playing members. The first officially sanctioned MCC women's team played its inaugural match the following May.

Heyhoe Flint said: 'I might be referred to as the catalyst, who in 1991 had the temerity to apply to become a member.'

She said she intended to be an active member, attending many matches and contributing in any other way possible.

At the ceremony to inaugurate the first women members Tony Lewis, the former England captain who had succeeded Ingleby-Mackenzie as MCC president, said: 'We are above all a cricket club. Women play cricket. So how can we be a cricket club without women? It's time for MCC to embrace both sexes.'

There are now over 600 women members of MCC with more than 1,000 on the waiting list.

The first ten female membes of MCC members were:

- Betty Archdale, who captained the first England women's team to tour Australia and New Zealand in 1934/35.
- Edna Barker, a former captain of South of England and Surrey, who toured Australia and New Zealand with England and won 15 caps in total.
- Audrey Collins, whose playing career began in the 1930s and continued for over four decades. She also served as president of the Women's Cricket Association from 1981 until 1993.
- Carole Cornthwaite, who played in 18 Test matches for England, and captained the team in 1986/87.

- Jackie Court, who played for England 40 times.
- Rachael Heyhoe Flint, who played for England from 1960 to 1979, gaining 45 caps and captaining the national team from 1966 to 1976.
- Sheila Hill, who played cricket for Oxford University, Kent and East England. She also umpired the final of the first Women's World Cup between England and Australia.
- Norma Izard, who was president of the Women's Cricket Association from 1994 to 1998. She also was England manager on 12 international tours.
- Diana Rait Kerr, curator of the MCC museum from 1945 until 1968.
- Netta Rheinberg, who was player/manager of the England tour to Australia and New Zealand in 1948/49 and was also secretary of the Women's Cricket Association.

42

Hansie Cronje's confession
stuns cricket *(2000)*

SOUTH AFRICA'S captain Hansie Cronje stunned the cricketing world when he confessed to accepting cash from a representative of an Indian betting syndicate in return for 'forecasting results'.

Although the truth about Cronje's actions had begun to leak out a few months earlier, his confession still sent shockwaves through the world of cricket. Until this moment the rumours of match-fixing in cricket had been speculation, lacking in hard evidence, and largely confined to the subcontinent.

Cronje's confession led to his sacking as South Africa's captain and exposed the full reach of the bookmakers. The report of India's Central Bureau of Investigation later in the year would make allegations against leading players from no fewer than eight of the nine Test-playing nations of the time.

The fact that it was Cronje who was involved made the shock greater still. The batsman was the captain of South Africa and one of the world's leading cricketers. He also professed to be a God-fearing Christian.

Four days before Cronje confessed and was sacked, the Delhi police had revealed they had a recording of a conversation between Cronje and Sanjay Chawla, who was acting on behalf of an Indian betting syndicate, over match-fixing allegations. Three other players, Herschelle Gibbs, Nicky Boje and Pieter Strydom, were also implicated.

The following day, the United Cricket Board of South Africa denied their players were involved in match-fixing. Cronje himself issued a strong denial, saying that 'the allegations are completely without substance'.

However, the denials failed to stand up to scrutiny for any length of time. In May 2000, the South African President Thabo Mbeki appointed Judge Edwin King to chair a commission of inquiry to look into match-fixing and other gambling-related matters.

The King Commission soon heard Gibbs testify that Cronje had offered him $15,000 to score less than 20 runs in a one-day international at Nagpur. Fast bowler Henry Williams had been offered $15,000 to concede more than 50 runs in that same match. In the event, Gibbs scored 74 off 53 balls and Williams injured his shoulder and couldn't complete his second over, so neither received the $15,000.

More was to follow as Cronje finally came clean about the extent of his involvement with the bookmakers, which dated back to 1996. That year, on a South Africa tour of India, he had been introduced to bookmaker Mukesh Gupta by Mohammad Azharuddin. Gupta gave Cronje $30,000 in an effort to persuade the South Africans to throw away their wickets on the last day at Kanpur and lose the match.

South Africa were already staring down the barrel of defeat in this match – they were 127/5 going into the final day and chasing 460. They were all out for 180.

Cronje, who did not bat on the final day, said he spoke to no other South African players and justified his actions because: 'I had received money for doing nothing.'

During the return tour later that year, Cronje also received $50,000 from Gupta for team information.

In addition, Cronje revealed that his actions in the 2000 Centurion Test, when he forfeited South Africa's second innings in order to make a game out of a match that had been ruined by rain, had been motivated by financial gain. A bookmaker called Marlon Aronstam contacted him offering R500,000 for the charity of his choice together with a gift if he could force a result.

A result was forced in that match, after Cronje offered England's Nasser Hussain a deal in which South Africa would declare on 248 before lunch, both teams would forfeit an innings, and England would have the rest of the day to try and win the game.

The tourists triumphed by two wickets thanks largely to Alec Stewart's knock of 73. At the time Cronje's actions were widely praised for turning a rain-soaked dead rubber into an exciting match.

After the match Aronstam visited Cronje, giving him cash payments of R30,000 and R20,000 together with a leather jacket. The promised gift of R500,000 to a charity never materialised.

As a result of his actions Cronje was banned for life from cricket while Gibbs and Williams were banned for four months each.

Meanwhile, the extent of the corruption in the sport was revealed by the Qayyum report into match-fixing, which was published in Pakistan. Saleem Malik and Ata-ur-Rehman were banned for life and six more players fined. Later that year the Indian Central Bureau of Investigation completed its own probe, which saw Azharuddin and Ajay Sharma banned for life while Ajay Jadeja and Manoj Prabhakar were banned for five years.

Azharuddin later saw his life ban overturned and it's possible the same would have happened to Cronje. He was already working to rehabilitate his reputation when he was killed in an accident on a private plane in 2002.

Conspiracy theories that Cronje was murdered on the orders of a cricket betting syndicate flourished after his death.

In August 2006, an inquest into the plane crash was opened by South Africa's High Court. The inquest concluded that 'the death of the deceased Wessel Johannes Cronje was brought about by an act or omission prima facie amounting to an offence on the part of pilots'.

At the time of Cronje's death, Nelson Mandela said: 'Here was a young man courageously and with dignity rebuilding his life after the setback he suffered a while ago. The manner in which he was doing that promised to make him once more a role model of how one deals with adversity.'

However, subsequent reporting on Cronje's involvement in match-fixing revealed that he had more than 70 bank accounts in the Cayman Islands which were illegal, because they were not declared to the South African Revenue Service.

The South African investigation was terminated at his death, but the implication of the multiple accounts was that the match-fixing was much more widespread than had been revealed to the King Commission.

Despite all this, Cronje finished 11th in a 2004 poll to find the 100 greatest South Africans, run by the South African Broadcasting Corporation. Many of the country's sporting public appear to have accepted Cronje's remorse when he said: 'I allowed Satan to dictate terms to me rather than the Lord.'

The spectre of gambling has proved difficult to exorcise from cricket. In 2010, the *News of the World* exposed another spot-fixing ring, between Salman Butt, Mohammad Amir and Mohammad Asif.

In October 2019, Bangladesh captain Shakib Al Hasan became the 26th player to be banned from international cricket for corruption, after failing to report an approach from a bookmaker.

Cronje concluded his King Commission statement by warning: 'As long as there is gambling on sporting events, legal or otherwise, players will continue to be approached, pressured and tempted.'

43

Marillier unveils the ramp shot *(2001)*

FEW SHOTS sum up the approach and technique of the modern batter more than the ramp shot and its close cousin the scoop shot.

First developed in the early 21st century, the shots require the batter to put their wicket and often their body, on the line in the search for runs. They are high-risk, high-reward strokes that are almost impossible to set a field for. The ramp and scoop shots embody the skill and all-out attacking mindset of modern batting.

The ramp shot was first played by Zimbabwean batsman Dougie Marillier, in a one-day international (ODI) match against Australia in Perth in 2001.

In the match at the WACA Ground, Australia had scored a formidable 302/5, a total that was underpinned by a superb 144 not out from Damien Martyn, who was batting on his home ground.

Australia reduced Zimbabwe to 91/3 from 19 overs before the tourists charged back with a record-breaking fourth-wicket partnership of 187 between Stuart Carlisle and Grant Flower.

A flurry of late wickets saw Marillier come in to bat with his side still needing to score 15 from the final over, which was to be bowled by Glenn McGrath, to win the match.

Marillier stunned spectators and commentators alike by moving outside the line of his off stump to flick the first ball over his shoulder on the full and send it to the fine leg boundary. He repeated the trick on the third ball, giving Zimbabwe hope of an incredible victory.

Marillier was unable to complete the job and his team lost by two runs. However, his innovation and execution of the two unorthodox boundary strokes caught the imagination of cricket fans, with the shot becoming known as the Marillier shot.

The following year, Marillier played the shot once again, this time with more success. His 56 not out powered Zimbabwe to a famous win against India in an ODI at Faridabad with the ramp shot sending Anil Kumble to the boundary.

The ramp shot requires a batter to position their body square-on with the ball and both feet pointing towards the bowler. The player then uses a horizontal bat to deflect the ball up, high over their shoulder and past the wicketkeeper towards the fine leg region.

It is a highly unorthodox and very risky method of scoring runs against deliveries pitched on a good line and length that are otherwise difficult to score from. It also sends the ball to part of the outfield rarely patrolled by a fielder and more often than not, goes to the boundary as it uses the bowler's pace for momentum.

As a calculated risk, the shot can frustrate the fielding side's captain, because positioning a fielder to stop a ramp shot may present gaps and scoring opportunities in other areas.

A variation of the ramp shot was played by Sri Lankan batsman Tillakaratne Dilshan, who first started to practise a scoop shot during his IPL stint with the Delhi Daredevils. Dilshan's Dilscoop was unveiled during the ICC World

Twenty20 in 2009. The shot is played by getting on one knee and scooping a short-of-a-length delivery over the keeper's head.

New Zealand's Brendon McCullum was another exponent of this shot with some calling it the McScoop in his honour.

The scoop shot differs to the ramp as it involves the batter ducking down into line with the ball and sending it over both his head and that of the wicketkeeper. It requires a degree of bravery as, especially against faster bowlers, a miss can not only result in the batter being dismissed, but also injury if the ball hits the batter.

The ramp and scoop shots may vary slightly in their execution, but there is no doubt they have added bold, attacking options to the batter's arsenal, characterising the attacking psyche of today's batters and entertaining cricket fans everywhere.

44

Edgbaston *(2005)*

Edgbaston, Birmingham, 4-7 August 2005
Second Ashes Test

England	Australia
407	308
Trescothick 90	Langer 82
Warne 4-116	Flintoff 2-52
182	279
Flintoff 73	Lee 43
Warne 6-46	Flintoff 4-79

England won by two runs

THE 2005 Ashes series has gone down in cricketing folklore as one of the greatest contests ever played between the old rivals of England and Australia. Cricket was on the front pages of the newspapers and millions were glued to Channel 4's television coverage as three Tests in a row went down to the wire.

There were outstanding individual performances from players on both sides before Kevin Pietersen's dashing century at The Oval gave way to wild celebrations. An open-top bus carried the England team through a packed Trafalgar Square before they were greeted by Prime Minister Tony Blair at 10 Downing Street.

It almost never happened, though. The thrilling second Test of the series at Edgbaston provided the closest finish of all and its finale proved pivotal. If Geraint Jones had not taken a tumbling catch to remove Michael Kasprowicz it would have all been different. If that delivery had taken a thicker edge off Kasprowicz's hand and run to the Edgbaston boundary Australia would have taken a 2-0 lead in the series and been almost guaranteed to extend their 16-year hold on the Ashes.

Australia had dominated during that period with England rarely able to compete. Even when England showed signs of improving they would come up short against Australia in the Ashes. That was the case once again in 2005 as coach Duncan Fletcher and captain Michael Vaughan had England on a firm upward trajectory.

However, Vaughan's men had been crushed by 239 runs in the first Test at Lord's as history threatened to repeat itself. This England team refused to go back into their shell though, instead opting to fight fire with fire.

'We went hard at them in the first Test, at Edgbaston we go harder,' Vaughan told his team.

The drama at Edgbaston started before play even began as Glenn McGrath – so often England's tormentor – trod on a cricket ball in the warm-up and tore his ankle ligaments. He was out of the match and England enjoyed a second slice of luck when a complacent Ricky Ponting ignored the loss of his best fast bowler and put England in to bat.

England took full advantage. Marcus Trescothick set the tone in the third over of the match as he smashed three boundaries off the bowling of Brett Lee. The England openers also both went after Shane Warne as the first session ended 132/1 at lunch. Trescothick fell short of his century but his 90 from just 102 balls had set the tone for the match. Pietersen and Flintoff hit rapid half-centuries as England racked up a first-innings total of 407 inside 80 overs.

Australia hit back and were 88/1 before Ashley Giles lured Ponting into a skied sweep shot. A steady stream of wickets followed with Giles accounting for Michael Clarke and Warne while Flintoff mopped up the tail as Australia were all out for 308.

The second day ended in astonishing fashion as Andrew Strauss was bowled while padding up to a Warne leg-break that turned two and a half feet.

The fireworks continued into day three as a blistering Lee spell reduced England's second innings to 31/4 before Flintoff counter-attacked brilliantly. The all-rounder scored 73 in a total of 183. This included a vital last-wicket stand of 51 with Simon Jones that featured a memorable pair of straight sixes. Australia were left needing 282 to win the match and take a huge step towards retaining the Ashes.

Australia's openers calmly reached 47 without loss while looking untroubled before Vaughan turned to Flintoff, who delivered his greatest-ever over. He bowled Justin Langer with the second ball before rapping Ponting's pads twice and seeing another take the Australian captain's edge but evade the slips. The sixth ball of the over was called a no-ball and Ponting could only snick the seventh to Geraint Jones behind the stumps and had to depart for a duck.

Matthew Hoggard, Giles, Flintoff and Simon Jones all chipped in with wickets to reduce Australia to 137/7 before Warne launched a counter-attack of his own. The leg-spinner hit Giles for two successive sixes as Australia moved to within 106 runs of victory.

The match swung back England's way on the final ball of the day as Harmison bamboozled Clarke with a superb slower ball to clean bowl the last recognised batsman.

Harmison said: 'I'm not sure where it came from, to be honest. My slower ball has been labelled by two of my former colleagues – Trescothick and Flintoff, who fielded at slip for my whole career – as the worst in the history of the game. But it worked that day and Clarke didn't pick it. We needed it.'

Edgbaston was packed again on the fourth morning despite the prospect of a short day's cricket. Lee and Warne added 45 before the latter stood on his stumps and fell to Flintoff. Lee then put on 59 with Kasprowicz, helped by Simon Jones spilling Kasprowicz at third man, as Australia moved on to 279/9, needing just three more runs for victory.

Australia almost won the game – and with it surely the series – when a Harmison full-toss was drilled through the covers by Lee and straight to Simon Jones, the only man out in the deep.

Jones said: 'It's weird. At the time I just got the long barrier down and stopped it. But I look back and think, "Jesus, ten yards either side and that would have been it, game over."'

Two balls later Harmison got a straight, rearing delivery to clip Kasprowicz's glove and Geraint Jones dived forward to take a near-hysterical match-winning catch, albeit one that brought a final twist.

England were level, having looked in massive danger of falling 2-0 behind, a result Vaughan has previously said would have been almost impossible to come back from.

Kasprowicz's wicket was the most decisive moment of all during a true Edgbaston epic that had swung back and forth wildly. The series was set up at 1-1 with three Tests still to play and plenty of drama still to come in one of the greatest Ashes contests of all time.

45

South Africa score 438 to chase down Australia *(2006)*

New Wanderers Stadium, Johannesburg, 12 March 2006
Fifth One-Day International

Australia	South Africa
434/4	438/9
Ponting 164	Gibbs 175
Telemachus 2-87	Bracken 5-67

South Africa won by one wicket

KNOWN BY many as the '438 match', the fifth one-day international (ODI) between South Africa and Australia in 2006 rewrote the record books and redefined what was possible for a batting side in 50 overs.

Ricky Ponting smashed 164 and led Australia to a world record score of 434 in the first innings but still ended up on the losing side. It was the first time that 400 had been breached in an ODI.

The record did not last long as Herschelle Gibbs outscored Ponting with 175 and South Africa eclipsed the Australian total to win a sensational match by one wicket.

The television commentators calling the match rated it the greatest ODI ever played, it set a host of records, and South Africa's 438 remains the highest second-innings total in the 50-over format.

The meeting at the New Wanderers was the decider in a five-match series. South Africa had won the first two games comfortably, but Australia fought back to win the next two.

The tourists had managed this comeback despite having to play the series without Glenn McGrath, whose wife was suffering from cancer. Shaun Pollock also missed the match, due to a back sprain.

This left both bowling attacks without their best fast bowler. The pair were sorely missed as the carnage unfolded and the captains struggled in vain to exert any control in the field.

Ponting won the toss and chose to bat with Adam Gilchrist getting the innings off to a flying start as he hit 55 off just 44 balls. At the other end his opening partner Simon Katich anchored the innings with a relatively sedate 79 off 90 balls. Katich was the only Australian batsman to end the match with a strike rate under 100.

Andrew Hall's diving catch removed Gilchrist and brought the Australian captain to the crease. Ponting proceeded to score his fastest century with 100 off 73 balls, and went on to his highest score at the Wanderers ground with 164 from 105 balls, including nine sixes and 13 fours.

Ponting and Katich put on 119 runs for the second wicket, before Katich was caught at third man by Roger Telemachus off Makhaya Ntini.

The wicket brought no respite for the Proteas as Michael Hussey, who had been promoted up the order, smashed 81 from just 51 deliveries before falling to Hall.

His captain followed shortly afterwards in the 47th over but Andrew Symonds and Brett Lee ensured the assault continued to the end of the innings. The 48th over began with Telemachus conceding 19 runs from four consecutive no-balls.

Telemachus finished with figures of 2-87 while Jacques Kallis saw his six overs disappear for 70 runs at an economy rate of 11.66 runs per over.

At the halfway point of the match South Africa were staring defeat in the face, which would mean they had squandered a 2-0 lead to lose the series 3-2. It was left to the unlikely source of Kallis to break the ice in the changing room with some humour.

The all-rounder said: 'Come on guys, it's a 450 wicket. They're 15 short!'

Coach Mickey Arthur valiantly tried to plan a run chase only to be ignored by his batsmen, who decided that all-out attack was their only hope of chasing down the formidable Australian total.

Captain Graeme Smith shook off the early loss of his opening partner Boeta Dippenaar to post a brutal 55-ball 90 that included 15 boundaries. The loss of Dippenaar brought a hungover Gibbs to the crease in the second over.

In his biography Gibbs revealed how he spent the previous evening overindulging at the bar, only returning to his hotel room in the early hours of the morning and almost missing the team bus.

Gibbs made light of his fuzzy head to star in a 187-run second-wicket stand with Smith before adding another 94 in the company of A.B. de Villiers.

He scored 175 runs off 111 balls, including 21 fours and seven sixes, to help turn an impossible position into a potentially winning one.

Gibbs was dropped on 130 by Nathan Bracken, who otherwise was the pick of the bowlers, taking 5-67, in a match that undeniably belonged to the batsmen. At the other end of the scale his team-mate Mick Lewis conceded 113 runs off his ten overs, the most runs ever conceded in an ODI.

When Gibbs was finally caught by Lee off the bowling of Symonds the score was 299/3 and work remained to be done. Kallis and Justin Kemp fell cheaply, leaving Mark Boucher to marshal the tail.

The wicketkeeper was aided by a brutal cameo from Johan van der Wath, who smashed 35 off 18 balls to reignite the run chase. Telemachus added a valuable 12 from six balls as the requirement dropped from a tricky 77 from 42 balls to a more achievable 36 from 22.

By the final over of the match, South Africa needed seven runs off six balls, with Boucher facing. A single brought Hall on strike and he hit a four before holing out, leaving the side at 433/9.

Ntini, the last batsman, deflected Lee's next delivery away for a single to third man to tie the scores and bring Boucher back on strike. The wicketkeeper sealed an astonishing victory with a lofted four over mid-on.

On the television commentary Tony Greig said: 'Straight down the ground, what a victory! That is a sensational game of cricket, and it is a superb victory. Well, I've been around the world watching this game ... look, there are tears, they are crying out there! The South Africans are charging out on to the field.

'Gilchrist shakes hands with Boucher. Ntini is on a high. Ponting cannot believe this has happened to his team. The South Africans at the Bullring today have seen the best one-day international ever played.'

The match set the tone for ODIs where passing 400 has become a frequent occurrence and teams are now targeting 500.

46

The IPL auction *(2008)*

TWENTY20 CRICKET is now a major part of the cricketing landscape with competitions around the world drawing huge crowds to grounds with millions more watching on television.

All major international tours now include at least one Twenty20 international match while franchise cricket provides riches for the best players in addition to colour and excitement for the spectators. The Indian Premier League's (IPL) dominates Twenty20 cricket attracting the world's best players, passionate crowds and huge television audiences.

There were several key landmarks in the rise of Twenty20 cricket to the place it has in today's game, but the IPL's inaugural auction in 2008 stands out as the moment when the sport of cricket changed forever.

The auction signalled not only the birth of the biggest, most lucrative and most popular cricket league in the world – it also gave the globe franchise cricket. It brought the best players from around the world together for a six-week extravaganza of cricket. In addition, the franchise system and the auction meant that every team and every player would now have a publicly assigned monetary value.

Twenty20 cricket began in 2003 as the brainchild of Stuart Robertson, the English Cricket Board's marketing manager, as the replacement for the Benson & Hedges Cup. A shorter format of the game was devised to deliver fast-paced, exciting cricket that was accessible to fans who did not have the time to follow the longer versions of the game. It aimed to attract a new, younger audience.

The first tournament between the English counties ended with Surrey Lions beating Warwickshire Bears by nine wickets in the final in front of a packed-out Trent Bridge. Attendances for the tournament topped a quarter of a million fans, over 150,000 more than had watched the previous season's edition of the Benson & Hedges Cup, making the tournament a success.

That success spawned Twenty20 leagues in South Africa, Pakistan and the West Indies, as well as one-off matches in Australia. The first Twenty20 international was played between New Zealand and Australia in 2005 while the schedule of that year's Ashes tour included a one-off Twenty20 international at the Rose Bowl in Southampton. The first ICC World Twenty20 followed in 2007 and was staged in South Africa.

However, India were reluctant to join the Twenty20 party. The first Indian Twenty20 league was not televised and the country's administrators had to be pressured into sending a team to South Africa for the inaugural Twenty20 World Cup. Even after agreeing to participate, India still went into the tournament rather half-heartedly. The Indian squad was missing a number of leading players, including Sachin Tendulkar, Sourav Ganguly, Anil Kumble, V.V.S. Laxman and Rahul Dravid.

The Twenty20 World Cup was exciting and unpredictable. West Indies batsman Chris Gayle set the tone with a boundary from the first ball of the tournament, Zimbabwe scored an upset win over Australia in the competition's fourth game and Yuvraj Singh plundered six sixes from one Stuart Broad over.

It was India who were crowned champions after knocking out Australia in the semi-finals and overcoming Pakistan in the final.

The IPL had been in the pipeline for a little while and had already had a formal launch. It was India's triumph as the first Twenty20 world champions that virtually guaranteed its success with a domestic audience when it began the following year.

The auction for the eight franchises themselves was held in January 2008 and fetched a total of $723.59 million. Mumbai Indians were the most expensive franchise with a $111.9 million price tag.

However, it was the players' auction that attracted most attention when it took place on 20 February 2008 in Mumbai.

Tendulkar, Ganguly, Dravid, Singh and Virender Sehwag were classified as icon players. They played for the franchises representing their home towns and hence did not enter the auction. This left Mahendra Singh Dhoni as the highest-profile Indian international available, his home town of Ranchi not boasting a franchise.

Dhoni duly became the most expensive player in the auction when he was bought by the Chennai Super Kings for $1.5 million. Australian batting all-rounder Andrew Symonds was the costliest foreign player when he was bought by Deccan Chargers for $1.35 million.

Elsewhere the auction threw up a few surprises. Eyebrows were raised amongst home fans when Kumble's price of $500,000 was eclipsed by a host of other Indian bowlers, notably the $900,000 that Kolkata Knight Riders paid out for the services of Ishant Sharma.

Australian all-rounder Cameron White went for $500,000 to Royal Challengers Bangalore. This made him more expensive than a host of his more illustrious international team-mates, including Shane Warne, Ricky Ponting, Glenn McGrath and Matthew Hayden.

Meanwhile, Pakistan's Mohammed Yousuf and South Africa's Ashwell Prince both suffered the embarrassment of going unsold.

'You want to know what you're worth – and you don't want to know what you're worth,' commented Australian bowler Nathan Bracken (who fetched a respectable $325,000).

It was Warne who proved to be one of the shrewdest buys of the auction. The Australian leg-spinner was the first player to be sold and surprisingly only went for his base price of $450,000 to the Rajasthan Royals. Warne went on to captain the Royals to the first IPL title as they defeated Dhoni's Chennai Super Kings in a final that went down to the last ball.

The IPL itself has gone on to become the behemoth of franchise cricket with a greater pull to some players than playing Test matches for their countries, such are the riches and prestige involved. It now has ten teams spread throughout India, seven in cities, three representing states. The franchises are now worth billions, thanks in large part to the 2022 broadcasting deal, which was worth $6.2 billion, second only in value to the NFL's deal.

Its success has seen similar formulas used for the Big Bash League in Australia, the Mzansi Super League in South Africa, the Caribbean Premier League and the Pakistan Super League. The Women's Big Bash League was started in 2015 by Cricket Australia, while the Kia Super League was started in England and Wales in 2016.

It was the format of Twenty20 cricket that made all this possible but it was the IPL's franchise formula, which utilised clever marketing strategies, that released the untapped commercial value of cricket around the globe.

47

The Lahore attack *(2009)*

WHEN EXTREMISTS opened fire on the Sri Lankan team bus in Lahore in 2009 cricket became a direct target of Islamic terrorism.

The bus was part of a convoy travelling to a Test match when it was hit. Six policemen and two bystanders were killed, as was the driver of the minivan carrying the match officials to the stadium.

No players were killed but seven members of the Sri Lankan team, the assistant coach, and the reserve umpire were all injured. It was the most serious attack on an international sports team since the Munich Olympics in 1972.

The attack marked the first time that cricketers had become the direct targets of terrorists, although they had previously been caught in the crossfire.

New Zealand's tours to Sri Lanka in 1987 and 1993 were both ended prematurely after suicide attacks came dangerously close to the tourists. The Kiwis were also in a Karachi hotel in 2002 that was hit by a suicide bomber, causing that tour to be abandoned.

In 2008, England's tour of India was disrupted by the Mumbai terror attacks. In fact, Sri Lanka themselves were only touring Pakistan as late replacements for India, who had pulled out of their tour following the Mumbai attacks. However, in these incidents cricket was collateral damage – in Lahore in 2009 the players were the primary target.

The aim of the terrorists was to isolate Pakistan from the rest of the world. Sport was a new target for the militants and they succeeded in preventing international cricket from being played in Pakistan for close to a decade. During that period, Pakistan were forced to host their home matches in the United Arab Emirates while the country also lost its planned matches for the 2011 Cricket World Cup.

The Lahore attack took place on 3 March 2009 as a convoy that included the Sri Lankan cricket team, match officials and security personnel travelled to the Gaddafi Stadium. The cricketers were on their way to the third day of the second Test against Pakistan.

They were attacked by 12 gunmen, believed to be part of a Jihadi group, near Liberty Square in the centre of Lahore. The gunmen showered the convoy in bullets, fired a rocket that narrowly missed the bus and threw a grenade that luckily exploded after the bus had passed over it.

The Pakistan police escorting the team returned fire and in the ensuing gun battle, six policemen and two civilians died. After about 20 minutes, the militants fled, leaving behind rocket launchers and grenades.

The driver of the Sri Lankan team bus, Mehar Mohammad Khalil, managed to keep on driving the bus for 500 metres until it reached the relative safety of the stadium. Khalil was later awarded the Pakistani honour Tamgha-i-Shujaat for his bravery.

The minivan carrying the match officials also came under attack with the driver killed and reserve umpire Ahsan Raza badly injured. The minivan was allegedly abandoned by security personnel. Match referee Chris Broad, the former England batsman, threw himself over Raza and kept his hand on his chest to slow down the bleeding from a bullet wound and may well have saved his life. A police officer, who climbed into the minivan seeking cover, drove the vehicle to safety.

Sri Lankan captain Mahela Jayawardene, vice-captain Kumar Sangakkara, batsmen Thilan Samaraweera and Tharanga Paranavitana, spinner Ajantha Mendis, and fast bowlers Chaminda Vaas and Suranga Lakmal all suffered minor injuries during the attack.

The Sri Lankan team were airlifted out of the stadium and immediate arrangements were made for them to return to Colombo on the next available flight. The second Test, which was the last scheduled fixture of the tour, was abandoned as a draw.

Off-spinner Muttiah Muralitharan was highly critical of the security provided to the Sri Lankan team.

He said: 'The security people we had didn't even seem to fight back. Were they professionals with enough training? They didn't seem to know what to do. I was surprised the terrorists were able to just reload the magazines and keep firing, and they never got caught. It was shameful. If this had happened in Colombo they would never have got away.'

The match officials, including Broad and umpires Steve Davies and Simon Taufel, were also critical of the security arrangements.

Taufel said: 'You tell me why no one was caught. You tell me why. Supposedly 25 armed commandos were in our convoy, and when the team bus got going again, we were left on our own.'

As a consequence of the attack, New Zealand cancelled their tour of Pakistan, which was scheduled for December 2009. It would take another ten years for Test cricket to return to the country. Pakistan's own tour of Bangladesh was also delayed in response to the attacks.

The fallout from the Mumbai and Lahore attacks combined with the Indian general elections to cast doubt over security arrangements for the 2009 Indian Premier League (IPL). In the end the whole tournament was moved to South Africa.

Pakistan was also scheduled to co-host the 2011 Cricket World Cup. In the wake of this attack on the Sri Lankan cricket team the International Cricket Council (ICC) stripped Pakistan of its hosting rights due to security concerns. The headquarters of the organising committee were originally situated in Lahore, but were then shifted to Mumbai.

In 2010, Pakistan hosted Australia on neutral grounds in England for a Test and one-day series. It was the United Arab Emirates that became the team's home from home and they hosted a number of tours there over their period in exile.

However, the atmosphere at the matches was sterile with stadia largely empty. The matches were a pale reflection of the noise, colour and passion of Pakistan's usual home support.

In 2017, international cricket made a tentative return to Pakistan with, fittingly, Sri Lanka leading the way when they played a Twenty20 match at the Gaddafi Stadium. That was followed by a one-day series two years later.

Finally, in December 2019, Sri Lanka agreed to play a two-match Test series in Pakistan, which marked the return of Test cricket to Pakistan over a decade since the terror attack had forced it into exile.

48

Cricket diplomacy brings PMs together *(2011)*

**Punjab Cricket Association Stadium, Mohali,
30 March 2011**

World Cup semi-final

India	Pakistan
260/9	231
Tendulkar 85	Misbah-ul-Haq 56
Riaz 5-46	Nehra 2-33

India won by 29 runs

THE MEETING of India and Pakistan in the semi-finals of the 2011 Cricket World Cup was one of the most hyped and watched cricket matches of all time.

The two countries had been rivals since they had gained independence from the British Empire in 1947 when they had been split by Partition. Since then the two nations have fought three wars and cricketing relations are frequently influenced by political or diplomatic tensions.

Following the Mumbai terrorist attacks in 2008, tensions were once again high between the two neighbours. The World Cup semi-final not only brought them together on the cricket pitch but helped thaw diplomatic relations too.

India's Prime Minister Manmohan Singh used the occasion to invite his Pakistani counterpart to the match and Yousuf Raza Gilani accepted.

The importance of the match was underlined by the official holidays declared in most of the states and provinces of the two countries. Thousands of television screens were installed in public places so fans could gather and watch the match together.

The stadium in Mohali was at full capacity for the match and in addition to the two prime ministers there were many more politicians, diplomats, VIPs and celebrities in attendance.

As the match approached tensions reached fever pitch, with some comparing the contest to a 'war' or talking about how the whole world would be watching India 'fighting' Pakistan on the pitch.

This hostility, along with the presence of the prime ministers and other notables, saw an unprecedented security operation put into place around the stadium. Fans were advised to turn up at least three hours in advance in order to pass through the security cordons.

On the pitch, India won the toss and elected to bat first with Virender Sehwag getting the home side off to a flying start. The opener hit nine fours in his quick-fire 38, and smashed 21 runs off Umar Gul in the third over of the innings.

His opening partner Sachin Tendulkar rode his luck to top-score in the India innings. Misbah-ul-Haq, Younis Khan, Kamran Akmal and Umar Akmal all dropped Tendulkar, three of them off the bowling of Shahid Afridi.

Tendulkar was finally taken by Afridi off the bowling of Saeed Ajmal for 85, which denied the 'Little Master' his 100th international century.

Wahab Riaz was the pick of the Pakistan bowlers, taking 5-46. He trapped Sehwag lbw and later took two wickets in two balls – Virat Kohli caught at backward point and Yuvraj Singh bowled – although he missed out on a hat-trick.

The wickets slowed down the Indian innings and after threatening a total of over 300 in the early overs India finished on 260/9 thanks to Suresh Raina shepherding the tail.

India's bowlers, backed up by a brilliant fielding effort, then suffocated Pakistan's batsmen to set up a 29-run victory. The Indians didn't give away an extra until the 37th over of the innings, and consistently put together strings of dot balls and tight overs to keep the pressure on the chasing team.

Yuvraj made up for his golden duck with a pair of wickets, but the most important breakthrough came when Harbhajan Singh bowled Umar Akmal for 29.

Akmal had struck a pair of sixes off Yuvraj and was looking dangerous but fell to the first ball of a Harbhajan spell. Afridi also fell to Harbhajan when he skied a catch off a full toss.

It was left to Misbah to steer the chase but he failed to score quickly enough. His 56 came off 76 deliveries and left Pakistan with far too much to do in the closing overs. He was the last man out, caught by Kohli off Zaheer Khan, as Pakistan were all out for 231.

The result sparked wild celebrations in India, which would be continued a few days later when they beat Sri Lanka in the final to clinch their second World Cup.

In Pakistan, the loss was met with violence and rioting while the team came in for criticism from fans and former players for their weak fielding and batting after a good showing earlier in the competition.

However, the significance of the match went far beyond the result with images of the two prime ministers watching it together beamed around the world.

The importance of this bit of cricket diplomacy was recognised by an Early Day Motion tabled in the House of Commons.

It read: 'That this House welcomes the success of India in its victory at the Cricket World Cup semi-final; notes the historic importance of the match between India and Pakistan, which was watched by more than a billion people; further notes the significance of the Indian and Pakistani prime ministers meeting at the match, the first time since the Mumbai terrorist attacks of 2008; and further welcomes the fact that the spirit of "cricket democracy" becomes an integral part of the countries' bilateral relations.'

49

Sandpapergate shakes cricket *(2018)*

WHEN AUSTRALIAN opener Cameron Bancroft was caught rubbing a small yellow object on the ball during a Test against South Africa it caused a scandal that shook cricket.

Bancroft initially said the object was sticky tape, but later it proved to be sandpaper. No Australian player had ever been charged with tampering before. Now, one had been caught cheating by the television cameras and few believed that the least-experienced player in the team had hatched this plot on his own.

The Australian captain Steve Smith and vice-captain David Warner were soon drawn into the scandal. They, along with Bancroft, were slapped with bans for the roles they played in the Sandpapergate plot to alter the condition of the ball in the Cape Town Test.

The incident sparked an immediate furore, extending well beyond cricket with Australian Prime Minister Malcolm Turnbull leading the condemnations.

The backlash also saw a number of high-profile figures in Australian cricket leave their jobs, while a review into the culture of Cricket Australia (CA) ended with the damning verdict that the organisation was 'arrogant'.

Australia had arrived in South Africa on a high after regaining the Ashes earlier in the year but the Test series between the two sides was controversial from the beginning.

During the first Test in Durban, Warner and Quinton de Kock were involved in an altercation in the players' stairwell during the tea break on day four, after the Proteas wicketkeeper allegedly made a remark about Warner's wife. In the same Test, Australian spinner Nathan Lyon was fined after dropping the ball on to A.B. de Villiers.

Tempers flared again in the second Test in Port Elizabeth with home seamer Kagiso Rabada given a demerit point after brushing shoulders with Smith while celebrating the batsman's wicket.

The series was level at 1-1 when the teams arrived in Cape Town for the third Test, which saw Warner abused by a spectator after being dismissed on day two. That incident was swiftly overshadowed by events on the third day.

Television cameras caught Bancroft rubbing a foreign object on the rough side of the ball. The coach Darren Lehmann then sent out a message through 12th man Peter Handscomb, following which Bancroft shoved a yellow object down his trousers, prompting scrutiny from the match officials.

At the press conference following the close of play, Bancroft and Smith admitted to ball-tampering with sticky tape, which later turned out to be sandpaper, in an effort to generate reverse swing and said 'the leadership group' had known about the plan beforehand.

Smith did not stipulate which players he meant but did insist that the coaching staff, including Lehmann, had no knowledge of the scheme. Smith and Warner were swiftly stood down from their roles for the remainder of the Test and then, along with Bancroft, suspended and sent home.

Heavier punishments were to follow with Smith and Warner banned by Cricket Australia for 12 months – a call that convinced the Board of Control for Cricket in India to also ban them from the Indian Premier League that season – and Bancroft hit with a nine-month ban.

CA found Warner to be responsible for initiating the plan to ball-tamper and he was told he would never again be considered for a leadership position within the team.

CA also explained that although Smith had not developed the plot he had failed to prevent it and taken part in the cover-up, so would not be eligible for a leadership role until a minimum of 12 months after his ban elapsed.

Bancroft received a shorter ban than his peers but also missed out on a county deal, with Somerset opting to tear up the agreement they had made with him the previous December.

Coach Lehmann was cleared of any wrongdoing but revealed his intention to stand down after the South Africa series.

He said: 'It is the right time to step away. I hope the team rebuilds and the Australian public can forgive the young men and get behind the XI.'

Later, an independent report found that CA had a 'win-at-all-costs' mentality that forced players to 'play the mongrel' and that Australian cricket had 'lost its balance and stumbled badly'.

In the wake of this, CA sacked high-performance manager Pat Howard and senior executive Ben Amarfio while CEO James Sutherland, chairman David Peever and board member Mark Taylor all resigned.

As well as bans from international cricket and the IPL, the incident hit Smith and Warner's bank balances as the pair saw sponsorship deals cancelled. Perhaps their greatest punishment was the shame of having let down family, friends, supporters and their country.

Smith said: 'To all of my team-mates, to fans of cricket all over the world, and to all Australians who are disappointed and angry. I want to make clear that as captain of the Australian cricket team, I take full responsibility. I made a serious error of judgement, and I now understand the consequences. It was a failure of leadership, of my leadership. I'll do everything I can to make up for my mistake, and the damage it's caused.

'If any good can come of this, if there can be a lesson to others, then I hope I can be a force for change. I know I'll regret this for the rest of my life. I'm absolutely gutted. I hope in time, I can earn back respect and forgiveness. I've been so privileged and honoured to represent my country and captain the Australian cricket team. Cricket is the greatest game in the world. It's been my life and I hope it can be again. I'm sorry and I'm absolutely devastated.'

50

The World Test Championship *(2021)*

The Rose Bowl, Southampton, 18–23 June 2021
ICC World Test Championship Final

India	**New Zealand**
217	249
Rahane 49	Conway 54
Jamieson 5-31	Shami 4-76
170	140/2
Pant 41	Williamson 52 not out
Southee 4-48	Ashwin 2-17

New Zealand won by eight wickets

THE PREMIER form of cricket finally got its first world champions in 2021, almost 150 years after the first Test had been played, and long after the shorter formats of the game had begun crowning global champions.

The World Test Championship was over a decade in the making. Initially proposed in 2009 and scheduled for 2013, it was cancelled two years later due to financial problems at the International Cricket Council (ICC). It was rescheduled for 2017 as a replacement for the 50-over Champions Trophy tournament but once again cancelled by the ICC.

Matches finally began with the 2019 Ashes series between England and Australia seeing points awarded to the participants and the final was scheduled for Lord's in 2021.

However, the onset of the Covid-19 pandemic meant not all the planned series took place while the final was eventually moved to the Rose Bowl in Southampton to enable a bubble environment.

The format of the tournament was also subject to much debate with differing proposals for play-off systems to determine the champions after an initial league stage. A timeless Test format was also considered as a possibility for the final as a means to avoid a draw and ensure a champion. In the end the ICC decided a reserve day would be sufficient to guarantee a result.

The 2021 tournament featured nine of the 12 Test-playing nations with the lowest-ranked trio of Afghanistan, Ireland and Zimbabwe missing out.

The ICC decided that the same number of points would be available from each series, regardless of series length, so that countries that played fewer Tests were not disadvantaged. It also decided that points would not be awarded for series results, but for match results only. These would be split equally between all the matches in the series, regardless of whether or not a match was a dead rubber, so that every match counted.

Due to the pandemic several series were postponed, so the final league standings were determined by percentage of points earned.

India and New Zealand qualified for the final as the top two teams in the league stage. New Zealand's place in the final was confirmed after Australia were forced to postpone their tour of South Africa while India beat England 3-1 to secure top spot in the table.

Both teams came into the final short of match practice. The Indian players hadn't played any cricket since the suspension of the Indian Premier League ten months earlier while New Zealand had played two Tests against England the previous June.

After losing the first day at the Rose Bowl to rain, New Zealand captain Kane Williamson won the toss on the second morning and put India in to bat. An opening partnership of 62 was ended when Kyle Jamieson had Rohit Sharma caught in the slips. Captain Virat Kohli and Ajinkya Rahane compiled a partnership of 61 but, after the skipper's departure with the score on 149, wickets fell steadily.

Jamieson was the pick of the New Zealand bowlers and his five wickets included the prize scalp of Kohli and the dangerous Rishabh Pant. Trent Boult took the final wicket of Ravi Jadeja as India were dismissed for a slightly below par 217 early in the afternoon of the third day.

New Zealand reached 101/2 by the end of the day's play with Devon Conway scoring the first half-century of the match before being dismissed by Ishant Sharma.

Rain meant that the fourth day's play was lost and the fifth day's start delayed. It also meant that the reserve day would almost certainly be required. When play did resume New Zealand made slow progress and lost three wickets before lunch to leave them on a precarious 135/5.

Williamson steadied the ship with a valuable 49, which alongside vital contributions from Jamieson and Tim Southee, took their total to 249, a first-innings lead of 32. Southee then struck twice to remove the Indian openers and leave them 64/2 at the close of play.

The sixth and final day began with India leading by 32 runs with eight wickets in hand. Jamieson struck early on removing Kohli for the second time in the match. Cheteshwar Pujara followed his captain back to the pavilion soon afterwards to leave India rocking on 72/4.

Pant led a counter-attack, scoring a quick-fire 41, while Mohammed Shami smashed 13 from just 10 balls.

The Indian innings finished on 170 all out, leaving New Zealand a target of 139 from 53 overs, far from easy in a slow-scoring match that had seen the bowlers on top. There was also the risk that the rain would return and bring the match to an early conclusion.

Ravi Ashwin gave India hope by removing both New Zealand openers before the 50 had come up, which brought Williamson and Ross Taylor to the crease. The class and experience of the pair shone through as they calmly put together a winning partnership of 98 in under 30 overs to clinch the trophy and become the first World Test champions.

As champions they received $1.6 million in prize money along with the ICC Test Championship mace, which they later took on a ten-city tour of New Zealand. The result also provided some compensation after the side's dramatic loss to England in the 2019 50-over World Cup Final.

Taylor said: 'I guess at the start of my career, there were a few ups and downs. We played in a few inconsistent sides, but, no, I guess over the last few years, the team has built into a fantastic, consistent side and after the heartbreak of the 2019 World Cup, this is definitely the highlight and I think probably makes up for that.

'Once the winning runs were hit, walking off with him [Williamson] and the discussions afterwards, it's something that I'll never forget. It was still touch and go when I went out there to bat; to get through that hard period and Kane's been a fantastic captain and ambassador for the game and our country.

'For him to be out there and on that last ball before, he sort of gave me a stare: "Hurry up and finish it," so that he doesn't have to. So it was nice to hit the boundary and celebrate what was a tough match with a lot of hard work over the last two or so years.'

In 2023, Australia became the second team to lift the mace, after beating India by 209 runs at The Oval. Having survived two cancellations and the Covid pandemic, the World Test Championship is now here to stay as a key part of the cricketing calendar.

Bibliography

Wisden Cricketers' Almanack, John Wisden & Co, various years 1864–2020

The Complete Encyclopaedia of Cricket, by Peter Wynne Thomas and Peter Arnold, Welbeck Publishing, 2007

A History of Cricket by H.S. Altham with E.W. Swanton, George Allen & Unwin, 1962

The Spirit of Cricket: A Personal Anthology by Christopher Martin-Jenkins, Faber and Faber, 1995

The Boundary Book Second Innings, compiled by Leslie Frewin, Spring Books, 1986

Guinness Cricket Firsts, Robert Brooke and Peter Matthews, Guinness Books, 1988

W.G. Grace: A Life by Simon Rae, 1998

Never Surrender: The Life of Douglas Jardine by Mark Peel, Pitch Publishing, 2021

Len Hutton, by Gerald Howat, Heinemann Kingswood, 1988

Who Only Cricket Know: Hutton's Men in the West Indies 1953/54 by David Woodhouse, Fairfield Books, 2021

The Packer Affair by Henry Blofeld, Readers Union, 1978

The Cricket War – the Inside Story of Kerry Packer's World Series Cricket by Gideon Haigh, Text Publishing, 1993

D'Oliveira: An Autobiography by Basil D'Oliveira, Collins, 1968

The D'Oliveira Affair by Basil D'Oliveira, Collins, 1969
Basil D'Oliveira – Cricket and Conspiracy: The Untold Story by Peter Oborne, Little, Brown, 2004
Time to Declare by Basil D'Oliveira, Dent, 1980
Twirlymen by Amol Rajan, Yellow Jersey Press, 2011
Cricket Around the World by Anton Rippon, Moorland Publishing, 1982

Websites
cricketarchive.com
cricinfo.com
bbc.co.uk/sport/cricket
thetimes.co.uk
theguardian.com
lords.org
ecb.co.uk
mcg.org.au
hambledon.cc